᠗᠗᠗᠗᠗᠗

GREEN BLADES RISING

᠗᠗᠗᠗᠗᠗

🝣🝣🝣🝣🝣

GREEN BLADES RISING

🝣🝣🝣🝣🝣🝣

By the same author

FOR CHILDREN
The Callow Pit Coffer
The Fire-Brother
The Green Children
Havelok the Dane
King Horn
The Pedlar of Swaffham
The Sea Stranger
Storm and Other Old English Riddles
Wordhoard
(*with Jill Paton Walsh*)

POEMS
The Rain-Giver
The Battle of Maldon and Other Old English Poems
(*translations; with Bruce Mitchell*)
Beowulf
(*translation; with Bruce Mitchell*)

TRAVEL
Pieces of Land: Journeys to Eight Islands

GREEN BLADES RISING

RISING

🔲🔲🔲🔲🔲🔲

THE ANGLO-SAXONS

🔲🔲🔲🔲🔲🔲

Kevin Crossley-Holland

A CLARION BOOK

The Seabury Press · New York

942.01
C 884

Library of Congress Cataloging of Publication Data

Crossley-Holland, Kevin.
  Green blades rising.

  "A Clarion book."
  Bibliography
  Includes index.
  SUMMARY. Analyzes Anglo-Saxon life and attitudes
through an examination of surviving prose and poetry,
sculpture, jewelry, and architecture.
  1. Anglo-Saxons—Juvenile literature.   2. England—Civilization—To 1066—Juvenile literature.
  1. Anglo-Saxons. 2. England—Civilization—To
1066. I. Title.
DA152.2.C76 1976   942.01   75-4576
ISBN 0-8164-3154-X

Printed in Great Britain

FOR RUTH

Now the green blade riseth from the buried grain,
Wheat that in the dark earth many days has lain;
Love lives again that with the dead has been:
Love is come again, like wheat that springeth green.
                    MEDIEVAL EASTER CAROL

᠊᠊᠊᠊᠊᠊

ACKNOWLEDGMENTS

᠊᠊᠊᠊᠊᠊

Acknowledgments are due to the following for permission to reproduce the colour and black-and-white plates: Aerofilms Limited, 10, 30; Ashmolean Museum, Oxford, *4, 5, 55*; The Trustees of the British Museum, *1, 2, 3, 7, 11, 13*, 6, 7, 12, 18, 22, 24, 25, 26, 28, 31, 33, 35, 36, 37, 38, 39, 40, 41, 42, 43, 45, 49, 52; Biblioteca Laurentiana, Florence, *9*; The Bodleian Library, Oxford, 27; Current Archaeology, 23; Dean and Chapter of Durham Cathedral, *12*, 46; Department of the Environment, 3, 4, 16, 21, 50; Guildhall Museum, 54; Michael Holford, *5, 6*; A. F. Kersting, 51; David Leigh, 29; Mansell Collection, 19, 20, 34; National Monuments Record, 11; Roman Baths Museum, Bath, *9*; Schleswig-Holsteinischen Landesmuseum, 1, 2; The Science Museum, 53; Sheffield City Museum, 8; Statens Historiska Museet, Stockholm, 13; The Board of Trinity College, Dublin, *10*; Universitetets Oldsaksamling, Oslo, 14, 15, 17; University Library, Utrecht, 48; Warburg Institute, 44; Winchester City Museum, 47. The copyright in plates *8* and *32* is held by the author.

I am most grateful to Professor Barry Cunliffe for providing me with the photograph of the Anglo-Saxon well at Portchester and to the Reverend Michael Crawshaw for allowing the font in Burnham Deepdale church to be photographed.

Acknowledgments are also due to Geoffrey Hill for permission to quote the first of his *Mercian Hymns*, André Deutsch, London, 1971; to R. S. Thomas for permission to reprint lines from 'Border Blues' in *Poetry for Supper*, Rupert Hart-Davis, London, 1958; and to Macmillan, London, who first published my own translations from Old English used in this book.

Finally, I must thank my father, as so often before, for his close and sensitive reading of the typescript and many valuable suggestions; Jill Paton Walsh for picking up errors of emphasis and sins of omission; Linda Kingston for typing the manuscript so accurately and swiftly; and above all my wife Ruth for her unfailing support, her innumerable critical suggestions, her maps and her organization of the picture research.

𝕾𝕾𝕾𝕾𝕾𝕾

CONTENTS

𝕾𝕾𝕾𝕾𝕾𝕾

ᘒᘒᘒᘒᘒᘒ

INTRODUCTION

ᘒᘒᘒᘒᘒᘒ

W HO were the Anglo-Saxons? What were they really like? What did they think about and talk about? No matter how many years pass, how many new influences may be absorbed and how much mechanical grabs may wreck, there remains, in the words of the poet who composed the great poem *Beowulf*

> many a fine sight
> for those who have eyes to see such things.

This book explores some of the poems and prose of the Anglo-Saxons, some of their illuminated manuscripts and sculpture, their jewellery, their architecture. To write about these 'sights' is also to write about you and me. More than half the words we use are Anglo-Saxon in origin; 'this book' is 'þis boc'. But it is not only words: our literature, our art, our laws, our villages and parish boundaries and, I believe, many of our attitudes owe much to the Anglo-Saxons.

'Go West young man' is a saying associated with the prosperous opportunities offered by the mid-West of the United States during the nineteenth century. But it could equally well apply to the dimly-lit Age of Migrations, for the Angles and Saxons had been moving westward, hungry for loot and new land, for perhaps 1500 years before they finally settled in England. Their original point of departure was probably the south Russian steppelands, just as it was for the other Germanic tribes like the Goths and Ostrogoths and Huns and Vandals and Franks, and just as it was for the Celtic peoples who began to settle in Britain and Brittany after 500 B.C. There are no reliable written records of the movement of the Germanic tribes; but archaeologists have discovered and dated a remarkable number of Germanic cemeteries, and in those cemeteries burial urns with buckles and brooches. These enable us to say that the Angles and Saxons lived in open and attractive farming country chiefly between the Rivers Elbe and Weser (see Map 1) at about the time of the birth of Christ.

'Anglo-Saxon' is a blanket name that covers the various Germanic tribes – principally Angles, Saxons and Jutes – who finally migrated to Britain during the fifth and sixth centuries A.D. The word 'England' derives from 'Angle'; the Scottish 'sassenach' and the Welsh 'saesneg', meaning stranger or Englishman, derive from 'Saxon'.

What were they like, our nameless distant ancestors who settled along and near the coast of North Germany? We can put together a jigsaw of evidence, bits and pieces from contemporary historians, Roman sculpture and later Anglo-Saxon poems that embody memories and traditions of earlier times. We can look with our own eyes, too, at Anglians of the first and fifth century (see plates 1 and 2). The Damendorfer Man seems to rest, his head outstretched on his arm. The Anglo-Saxons often referred to the dead as sleeping:

> Man must go to the grave that awaits him . . .
> and his body, rigid on its clay bed,
> will sleep there after the banquet.

The Windeby girl and Damendorfer Man are compelling but limited in what they can tell us. Sculptures of German tribes on the column of Marcus Aurelius in Rome give us a more detailed picture: men with long hair and trim beards, knee-length shirts, cloaks buckled at the right shoulder, and ankle-length trousers; women with hair longer yet and long sweeping dresses; a village of little dome-shaped huts.

But we must above all turn to Tacitus, the great first century

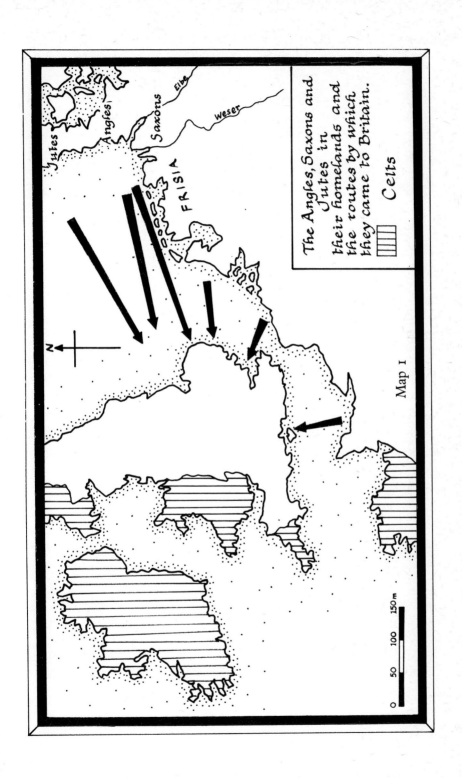

The Angles, Saxons and Jutes in their homelands and the routes by which they came to Britain.

Celts

Jutes

Angles

Saxons

Elbe

Weser

FRISIA

N

Map I

0   50   100   150 m

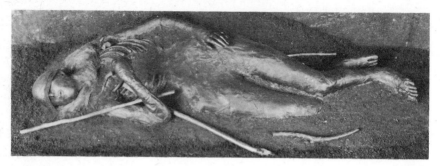

1. A fair-haired, fourteen-year-old girl of the 1st century found in the bog at Windeby in Schleswig. She was blindfolded and sacrificed to the Mother Goddess in a fertility rite.

Roman historian who provides in his *Germania* a detailed picture of the way of life of the German tribes within the Roman Empire. Even his description of clothing tells us more than Damendorfer Man and the sculptures on the column of Marcus Aurelius: the robe worn tight and showing the shape of every limb; cloaks often made from animal pelts mottled 'with patches of the spotted skin of beasts that live in the outer ocean and the unknown sea'; a woman's dress including 'undergarments of linen, embroidered with purple, and, as the upper part does not extend to sleeves, forearms and upper arms are bare. Even the breast, where it comes nearest to the shoulder, is bare.'

2. This 5th century man was found pressed, as a flower is pressed, in the bog at Damendorf in Schleswig. His skin was preserved but chemicals in the peat had melted his bones. His clothes lay at his feet.

Tacitus took a poor view of the peacetime activities of the Germanic tribesmen. He portrays the 'grim warriors' involved in an endless round of hunting, idling, gluttonous feasting and sleeping, 'while the care of the house, hearth and fields is left to the women, old men and weaklings of the family.' This picture, so reminiscent of the after-lives of Norse warriors in Valhalla, reads like an exaggeration. Perhaps it is true of a very small minority – the chiefs and their companions.

This minority was, however, the heart of a Germanic tribal society, and evolved its most characteristic attitudes. Tacitus makes two crucial observations:

> As for leaving a battle alive after your chief has fallen, that means lifelong infamy and shame. To defend and protect him, to put down one's own acts of heroism to his credit – that is what they really mean by allegiance. The chiefs fight for victory, the companions for their chief.

and

> A man is bound to take up the feuds as well as the friendships of father or kinsman.

These passages stress the bond of chief and follower and the bond of kinship, valour, and the blood feud. And these were the central preoccupations not only of the Germanic tribes but also of their descendants, the Anglo-Saxons. They were just as important to Anglo-Saxons at the Battle of Hastings in 1066 as to Germanic warriors in the first century.

But the tribesmen described by Tacitus were mainly farmers, not warriors. The pattern of life for most of them was determined by the seasons. It is significant that the chief God at this time was not yet the warlike Woden but Erce or Nerthus, Mother Earth. Tacitus tells us this, and a 'Charm for Land-Remedy', composed in eighth-century Christian England, contains a memory of the old pagan belief. The incantation begins with the words, 'Erce, Erce, Erce, eorþan modor' (earth mother), and part of the charm goes:

Then let the plough be driven forth and the first furrow made.
Then say:

> 'Hail to thee, Earth, mother of men!
> Be fruitful in God's embrace,
> filled with food for the use of men.'

In thinking about both the Germanic tribesmen and Anglo-Saxons, we should celebrate the unsung ploughman. He provided the food; and when it was a matter of fighting, he and his like were summoned and provided the greater part of the army. We are concerned above all with an agricultural people.

The zenith of the Roman Empire was the second century A.D. Stretching east to Asia Minor and west to Spain, north to Britain and south to Egypt, it called for outstanding administration to hold it together. The wonder is that it did hold for so long. The subject tribes, and above all the Germanic ones, were always on the look-out for a chance to regain lost independence and salvage lost pride. At the end of the century there are reports of Saxon pirates harassing the coast of Gaul, and allying themselves with the self-interested Roman Carausius who inspired the revolt of the Classis Britannica (the British fleet) and established himself for seven years as 'Emperor of Britain'. Above all, the building of the massive Roman shore forts, such as those at Richborough, Reculver, Pevensey and Portchester (see plate 3) protecting the east and south of England, still reminds us today how seriously the Romans took the threat of the sea-going Frisians and Saxons (see Map 1).

But it was in the fourth century that Roman control over Britain was taxed and lost. In 360 Scots from Ireland and Picts from Scotland overran Hadrian's Wall (see plate 4) and raided the north country; in 364 Saxons molested the southern or so-called Saxon shore, and in 367 the Count of the Saxon Shore was slain; in 383 a considerable section of the Roman troops in Britain revolted and crossed over to Gaul, in support of a British commander who claimed he was the rightful Emperor. Then in 395, after the death of Theodosius, the Roman Empire itself was

3. The Roman walls and bastions of the Saxon shore fort at Portchester in Hampshire. They still stand to a height of 20 feet.

4. A section of Hadrian's Wall near Housesteads.

cut into two by claim and counter-claim to the succession. At precisely the time when Britain was tottering and Germanic tribes were gathering to strike at the heart of the Empire itself, the Western Provinces (which included Britain) were entrusted to Honorius, a child, who 'remained till his death in 423 childish in mind, without wisdom or capacity, a breeder of pigeons'.*

Three troop withdrawals at the turn of the fourth and fifth centuries left Britain hopelessly exposed to Picts, who were carrying away thousands of hostages, to Scots and Saxons. The reason for the withdrawals was to shore up Gaul, which was under terrible pressure from the Germanic tribes who had over-crowded the land between the Rivers Elbe and Weser, driven south and taken over low-lying Frisia, and still hungered for more land. Despite repeated and frantic pleas for assistance, the Romano-Britons were in 410 finally cut off from imperial govern-ment and left to fend for themselves. The fifth century chronicler Zosimus wrote:

> The barbarians from beyond the Rhine (i.e. the Saxons) ravaging everything at pleasure compelled both the inhabitants of the British Isle and some of the peoples of Gaul to secede from the Empire of the Romans and to live independent of them, no longer obeying the Roman laws.

It seems likely that in 446 the Britons made a final unsuccessful plea for help to Aetius, Commander of the Roman troops in Gaul. Desperate for help against both Picts and Scots, one British leader (possibly Vortigern) then invited a Saxon leader (possibly Hen-gest) to bring a number of warriors into Britain as mercenaries (see page 26 for a more detailed description). But many of those who came to fight stayed to settle; they summoned their families, their friends, in hundreds and thousands. In the middle of the fifth century, the Angles and Saxons and Jutes (henceforth, Anglo-Saxons) began to see England not as a regular hit-and-run victim but as a possible home.

The long narrow boat of the Anglo-Saxons had too shallow a

---

* R. H. Hodgkin: *A History of the Anglo-Saxons.*

keel to support a mast and canvas. It was propelled by oarsmen, up to twenty-eight of them, and steered by a large paddle in the stern. In boats such as this, which held up to forty additional passengers, the migrants crossed the choppy sea from the north of Germany to the south and east shores of Britain.

What did they find? In the fifth century, Britain was still an almost silent place. Between small communities lay great forests of ash and oak and beech, such as the Weald which stretched from Hampshire to Kent and was 120 miles long and 30 miles wide, and Selwood, and Wychwood, and Sherwood, and the Chilterns; then there was misty moorland, especially in the west country, and around York; there was heathland, like that about Grimes Graves; and there was marshland such as the Fens and in Somerset and around Romney. Only two or three out of every 100 potentially arable acres had been reclaimed.

Through this empty land the Anglo-Saxons would have been delighted to discover 5000 miles of expertly-made, usually straight roads, built and used by the Roman army. This was the network that linked the 12 tribal capitals, 33 civil towns and estimated 2500 self-sufficient villas built by the Romans during their 500 years of occupation. But only three towns, London, York and Winchester, had a population in Roman times of over 10,000. It is thought, in fact, that the entire population of Britain at this moment amounted to about half a million: that is to say, a city the size of present-day Bristol or Manchester.

Many places the Anglo-Saxons came to had already been raided during the previous ninety years. Villas had been destroyed; garrisons had dwindled and been deserted; and most of the towns, their trade routes threatened, were in decline.

So the Anglo-Saxons came, in effect, face to face with the 'barely Romanised country folk', the British living in small settlements in the east of England and hilltop villages and forts in the west. Tradition has it that the British found incomparable leadership for a while in Arthur (see page 28 for more detailed description), stemmer of the tide and winner of twelve great battles between Christian Celt and pagan Saxon. But this was a time of misery for the British. A Welsh monk, Gildas, not to be relied on in all cases but probably reliable in this, speaks of 'the groans of the Britons' who appealed in vain one last time to the Romans in Gaul. Of the suffering Britons Gildas says: 'Repellunt barbari ad mare, repellit mare ad barbaros.' The barbarians drove them to the sea, the sea drove them back to the barbarians.

WAR

☖☖☖☖☖

WEAPONS

☖☖☖☖☖

THE Anglo-Saxons' idea of beauty was not the same as ours. It is true they responded to magnificent desolate places, and to the first call of the mournful cuckoo in spring; but their pleasure in an illuminated manuscript or a tapestry was not only in the way it was made but also in its function. We do not necessarily associate usefulness and beauty; the Anglo-Saxons almost invariably did. They admired well-wrought jewellery – brooches, buckles, clasps, purses – all of them functional things. They adorned their drinking horns, they hammered and decorated fine silver plates and bowls. They made elaborate stone crosses and grave headstones. But above all, they delighted in beautiful weapons.

No objects matter as much to us today as his weapons mattered to an Anglo-Saxon warrior. Where he went, they went. The *Beowulf*-poet says:

> They set their bright battle-shields
> at their heads. . . . Placed on the bench
> above each retainer, his crested helmet,
> his linked corslet and sturdy spear-shaft
> were plainly to be seen. It was their habit,
> both at home and in the field,
> to be prepared for battle always. . . .

Sword and scramasax; shield and spear; helmet and coat of mail: there is no escaping them in the literature, jewellery, manuscript illumination, sculpture or archaeological remains of the

Anglo-Saxons. Before establishing how the Anglo-Saxons first swept through the country, then tore at each other's throats, vied with the Vikings for two and a half centuries, and were finally overwhelmed by the Normans, let us look more closely at the unchanging instruments of this long chronicle of death and defence.

The sword was certainly the king of weapons. To own a sword at all implied standing and wealth, and the gift of a sword was the most potent symbol of the bond between a lord and his follower.

> A crowd of pale faces fell to the earth. The raven wheeled,
> dusky, dark brown. The gleaming swords so shone
> it seemed as if all Finnesburh were in flames.*

The most famous swords had lineages of famous owners, which made them all the more valuable; they also had names, such as 'Nægling', Beowulf's own sword, which snapped in his fight against the dragon; and sometimes they were engraved (as were rings) with runes, letters from an alphabet of twenty-four letters known as the futhark, which had secret meanings and were believed to give special protection. After land and livestock, a sword was probably the most important possession that a man could bequeath. In the earliest surviving will made by an English king, King Alfred makes mention that he leaves 'to Ealdorman Ethelred a sword worth 100 mancuses'.

The best of Anglo-Saxon sword blades were springy, and they were all between two foot six inches and two foot nine inches long. Some were decorated with ornamental patterning, some carried the name of their maker, some bore a magical inscription designed to protect the owner. A sword found at Lincoln is inscribed: ANTANANANTANANTAN. What can this mean? Does it contain, perhaps, an echo of the music of swords in battle? Was it some age-old formula murmured by a warrior before going into the fight, just as men chanted 'Erce, Erce, Erce, eorþan

---

* Lines from 'The Finnesburh Fragment'.

5. The Abingdon Sword. 9th century.

modor' before casting seed into the soil, and just as some people today cross themselves or genuflect when first facing the altar in a church? The finest decoration on a sword was, however, reserved for the hilt. The superb metalwork of the Abingdon sword (see plate 5) or the pommel found at Fetter Lane in the City of London (see plate 6) 'decorated with whirling snakes interspaced with a leaf pattern'* has not been bettered in any later age.

Those warriors who did not own swords probably made do with a scramasax. That sounds nasty, and so it was: a single-edged knife anything from 3 to 30 inches long, carried in a sheath suspended from the belt. But for the great majority of Anglo-Saxons the principal weapons were the spear and the shield.

> When the sea-stained travellers
> had reached the hall itself in their fearsome armour,
> they placed their broad shields
> (worked so skilfully) against Heorot's wall.
> Then they sat on a bench; the brave men's
> armour sang. The seafarer's gear
> stood all together, a grey-tipped forest
> of ash spears. . . .

* D. M. Wilson: *The Anglo-Saxons.*

6. The Fetter Lane sword pommel. 9th century.

As *Beowulf* indicates, spear-shafts were made of ash wood. Time's hunger is not so great for metal as for wood, and archaeological discoveries have shown that the socketed tips of the spears were made of iron and usually leaf-shaped.

Surrounded as they were by vast forests, the Anglo-Saxons were sensitive to the way in which wood had a life of its own. In one short riddling poem, a tree laments the way in which it has been 'treated most terribly' and is 'sorely wounded, and sullen in its chains'; this is a battering-ram. Another riddle begins

I'm by nature solitary, scarred by spear
and wounded by sword, weary of battle.
I frequently see the face of war, and fight
hateful enemies. . . .

The answer is a shield. The circular or kite-shaped, curved
shield of wood with an iron boss was the most common weapon
of defence. It was the shield that stood between man and sword,
man and axe, man and 'the iron-tipped arrow shower', all of
them portrayed so vividly in the Bayeux Tapestry. And like the
sword, a shield declared its owner's wealth (see plate 7).

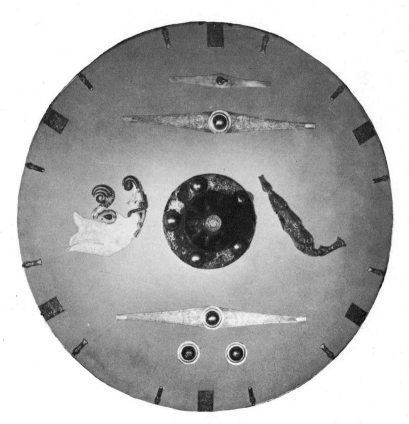

7. A reconstruction of the shield found in the Sutton Hoo ship-burial.
7th century. It was made of lime wood covered with oak-bark tanned hide,
on which were mounted ornaments – a stylized dragon, a bird of prey and a
heavily decorated boss.

Fortunate warriors had two other defences. One was the mail shirt, made of linked iron rings, which does not seem to have been widely used in Britain. In *The Anglo-Saxons*, D. M. Wilson writes:

> . . . suits of mail must have been expensive to make and were obviously worn only by leaders and chieftains, a leather jerkin being sufficient protection for the more humble members of society. The mail-shirt would itself be worn over a leather jerkin or even over a padded vest, so that the interlocking rings might not be driven into the flesh when pierced.

The other defence was the helmet which, like the sword and shield, could well be a very beautiful object in its own right. The helmet found in the seventh century royal ship-burial at Sutton Hoo (see colour plate 1) was made of iron, to which was added in bits of cast bronze 'a modelled nose and mouth with toothbrush moustache and a pair of eyebrows'. It was superbly panelled with detailed, decorative scenes probably evoking heroic history and invoking divine protection, and it would have been padded inside with wool or leather scraps.

In one scene from *Beowulf*, warriors march to the great hall Heorot:

> Then they hurried on. The ship lay still;
> securely anchored, the spacious vessel
> rode on its hawser. The boar crest, brightly gleaming,
> stood over their helmets: superbly tempered,
> plated with glowing gold, it guarded the lives
> of those grim warriors.

The boar-crest, symbol of heroism in both pagan Anglo-Saxon and Celtic societies, can be seen to perfection in the helmet found at Benty Grange in Derbyshire (see plate 8); the bronze boar is decorated with silver studs, perhaps representing bristles, and it has gold and garnet eyes. But this helmet is all the more remarkable for the Cross embedded in its nosepiece. It thereby embodies both the fatalism of the heroic code, in which man's greatest ambition was to achieve fame in this life, and optimistic Christianity with its message of life after death.

8. The Benty Grange helmet. The gaps between the iron bands were originally filled in with horn plates. 7th century.

One could write of the archer, or the axeman, but these were exceptions not commonplace in Anglo-Saxon warfare. The sword and the helmet for the leaders of men, the spear and the shield for all, that is how things were, and they could wreak ghastly destruction:

> They hurled their spears, hard as files,
> and sent sharp darts flying from their hands.
> Bow strings were busy, shield parried point,
> bitter was the battle. Brave men fell
> on both sides, youths choking in the dust.*

> * Lines from 'The Battle of Maldon'.

AGAINST THE ROMANO-BRITISH

IN 'The Second Coming', W. B. Yeats wrote:

> Things fall apart; the centre cannot hold;
> Mere anarchy is loosed upon the world . . .

When the Romans withdrew from Britain, an anarchic situation developed which was exploited by any number of ambitious British, less interested in maintaining anything of the old administrative systems than in grabbing power for themselves; the once-unified country reverted to its old tribal divisions (see plate 9). These little kingdoms vied with each other, and had also to face their common enemy, the Picts.

This is the background to the arrival of the Anglo-Saxon *foederati*, or mercenaries – an event of great historical significance noted by Gildas and also by the great Northumbrian historian, the Venerable Bede, who was writing around the year 700 but drawing on earlier (and now lost) material. *The Anglo-Saxon Chronicle*, too, notes:

> 449. . . . Vortigern invited the Angles hither, and then they came hither to Britain in three ships at a place called Ebbsfleet. King Vortigern gave them land to the south-east of this land on condition that they fought against the Picts.

One payment for mercenaries was cash; another was land. It is not surprising that the land-hungry Anglo-Saxons should have chosen green acres, fertile fields somewhere near the Kent coast. Gildas chides Vortigern for offering land at all, and calls him a

9. Gorgon's Head from the pediment of the Roman temple at Bath. The moustache and flying hair suggest, however, a Celtic warrior – the kind met by Romans and Anglo-Saxons alike.

tyrant for doing so, but this practice was not at all unusual. Exactly the same arrangement in 912 first gave the Norsemen a foothold in Normandy.

But the entry for 455 in *The Chronicle* reads:

> In this year Hengest and Horsa fought against King Vortigern at a place called Aylesford, and his brother Horsa was slain. And after that Hengest succeeded to the kingdom and Æsc, his son.

So servant had turned master. But it would be wrong to pay too much attention to one group of men in one place at one time, or to think of the Angles, Saxons and Jutes as any kind of unified force. What happened was that from the middle of the fifth century, small groups were crossing the water from the north of Germany and settling in Lincolnshire, Norfolk, Suffolk, Essex, Kent and Hampshire; that is to say, all the way from the River Humber to the Solent. Soon after this they were sailing through the Fens and settling in Cambridgeshire and sailing up the Thames into Buckinghamshire and Oxfordshire.

In some places the British held their ground and fought back, building sandcastles destined to collapse before the endless incoming tide of men; in other places they probably made tactical withdrawals; and archaeological evidence proves there were some places where British and new settlers lived uneasily side by side – the British on the light soil of hill-slopes and the Anglo-Saxons, who preferred a clay soil for their ploughs, in the valleys.

Some time between 490 and 503 – the exact date is uncertain – the British made an organized attempt to resist the settlers. Bede writes:

> Their leader at this time was Ambrosius Aurelianus, a modest man of Roman origin, who was the sole survivor of the catastrophe in which his royal parents had perished. Under his leadership the Britons took up arms, challenged their conquerors to battle, and with God's help inflicted a defeat on them. Thenceforward victory swung first to one side, and then to the other, until the battle of Badon Hill, when the Britons made a considerable slaughter of the invaders.

The encounter at Badon Hill, or Mons Badonicus, seems to have arrested the advance of the Anglo-Saxons for perhaps two generations: fifty years. This is the time to which the historical figure of Arthur, greatest of all English heroes in myth and legend, belongs. Who was he? The work of scholars and archaeologists is unlikely ever to define precisely this shadowy figure who has haunted the British imagination for so long; the sources are simply too few. Some scholars believe he *was* the Ambrosius Aurelianus to whom Bede refers. In his *History of the Britons*, Nennius, a ninth century Welsh monk, drawing on earlier traditions, does associate Arthur and Mons Badonicus in his description of the twelve great battles fought and won by Arthur:

> The twelfth battle was at Badon Hill, where nine hundred and sixty men perished at one charge of Arthur's and no-one killed them save he himself. And in all the battles he was victor. And they, when they were defeated in all the battles, sent for help to Germany, and their numbers were ceaselessly added to, and they brought kings from Germany to rule over those in Britain.

There has been much speculation as to where Badon is situated. Is it perhaps Badbury Rings in Dorset (see plate 10), a most impressive Iron Age hill-fort beside a Roman road?

It is partly because so little is certain about Arthur that he is so compelling. Some say he was Ambrosius Aurelianus, some that he was a Northern prince to whom victory at Mons Badonicus was only later attributed; in *The Figure of Arthur*, Richard Barber has argued that he was a prince of the Irish colony of Dalriada in the south-west of Scotland. Certainly it is known that 300 mounted warriors from Dalriada carried out a heroic but disastrous raid on the Anglo-Saxons at Catraeth (Catterick) in Yorkshire, and in the poem *The Gododdin* recording the event, there is mention of a man's bravery 'though he was not Arthur'. *The* Arthur?

> Three hundred golden-torqued men attacked:
> Contending for the land was cruel.
> Although they were being slain, they slew;
> Till the world ends, they will be honoured.
> Of the comrades who went together,
> Tragic, but a single man returned.★

★ Lines from 'The Gododdin' in *The Earliest Welsh Poetry* by Joseph P. Clancy.

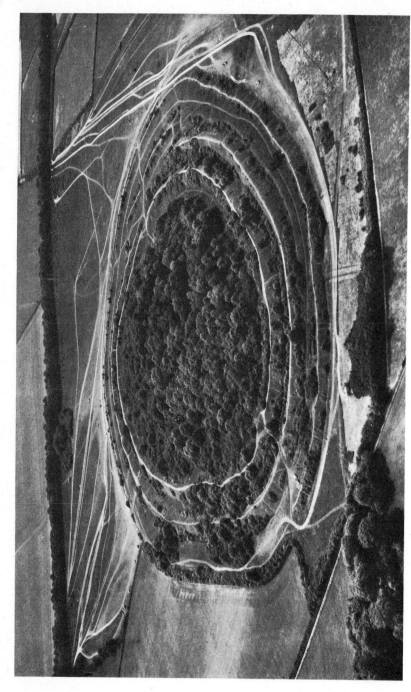

10. Badbury Rings, Dorset.

So the attack at Catterick failed; other attacks failed; and slowly the Romano-British resistance petered out, largely for lack of any systematic organization. The Anglo-Saxons advanced and we can say that in the second half of the sixth century England became irreversibly Anglo-Saxon. In 552, two substantial groups of warriors from Hampshire and from the upper Thames valley converged, joined forces and moved south and west, more or less as they willed. Twenty-five years later the Cotswolds fell under Anglo-Saxon control, with the effect that the British in the south-west were cut off from those in Wales; away to the north Anglo-Saxons moved from Yorkshire to the Tyne Valley and then to Bamburgh, which was to become the capital of the first great Anglo-Saxon kingdom, Bernicia; and in the great body of the south and east of England, the Anglo-Saxons consolidated their hold.

We know that many Britons remained in Anglo-Saxon territory: some clung to their upland farms; others were taken into slavery, and the Anglo-Saxon word for the Welsh, 'wealas', also means slaves. But for the most parts the Celts were being forced relentlessly away west, to Scotland, to Man, to Wales, to the Cornish peninsula, and to Ireland and Brittany, where they have since remained.

Of course the struggle between Celt and Saxon continued fitfully: in the late eighth century Offa's dyke was built as a frontier against the Welsh (see plate 11); in 937 Athelstan of Wessex beat a combined force of Celts and Norsemen at Brunanburh. Indeed the struggle still continues. One has only to think of the wars of the Middle Ages, the long tormented history of Ireland, the self-government of Man, the present Nationalist parties and policies, to recognize that Englishman and Celt are not and never will be well-adapted partners. The Anglo-Saxons and their descendants organize and act; they are not, on the whole, so very imaginative. The Celts have a passionate dream of past and future, and never quite realize it:

We are not English . . . *Ni bydd diwedd*
Byth ar sŵn y delyn aur.

11. Offa's Dyke. 8th century.

Though the strings are broken, and time sets
The barbed wire in their place,
The tune endures; on the cracked screen
Of life our shadows are large still
In history's fierce afterglow.*

* R. S. Thomas: Lines from 'Border Blues' in *Poetry for Supper*, Rupert Hart-
Davis, London 1958. The Welsh words mean: there will never be an end to the
sound of the golden harp.

The Sutton Hoo helmet, newly reconstructed from hundreds of corroded iron fragments found in the [shi]-burial. 7th century.

The Sutton Hoo Purse-lid. The material of this [sum]ptuous lid was bone or ivory, decorated with [gar]nets and gold. The outer pair of plaques at the [bot]tom show a man between two rampant animals; [the] inner pair show a bird of prey attacking a duck. [7th] century.

The Sutton Hoo Belt-buckle. This is the heaviest [soli]d gold object ever found in England – it weighs [20] ounces. The beauty of the flat interlacing animal [pat]terns makes the gold buckle the most artistically [sati]sfying of all the great finds at Sutton Hoo. [7th] century.

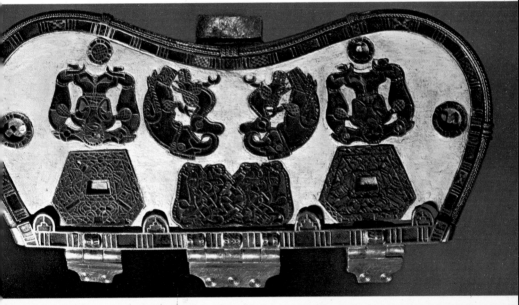

5. The Alfred Jewel. It is made of gold, and a crystal plaque covers an enamelled figure of a man holding two sceptres. The inscription round the edge reads +AELFRED MEC HEHT GEWYRCAN: Alfred ordered me to be made. 9th century.

6. An Anglo-Saxon burial urn found in East Anglia. 6th century.

4. Part of St Cuthbert's stole, showing St Peter. 10th century.

🔁🔁🔁🔁🔁🔁

AGAINST EACH OTHER

🔁🔁🔁🔁🔁🔁

A T the end of the sixth and beginning of the seventh centuries, the Anglo-Saxons grouped into seven small kingdoms known as the Heptarchy (see map 2). The first kingdom to gain the ascendancy was Kent, at just the time when Augustine was despatched by Pope Gregory on his mission to Britain. The King of Kent, Æthelbert, was recognized by neighbouring leaders as the Bretwalda, or ruler of Britain, a title which shuttled from kingdom to kingdom during the following two centuries. It is far from certain what power the Bretwalda had. We know Æthelbert arranged safe conduct for Augustine from Kent to somewhere in the midwest of England; we know, too, that subordinate kings sometimes met at an overlord's court, and there granted him parcels of land from their own kingdoms. The power of the Bretwalda clearly depended on the strength of each individual who held it; all in all, a kind of limited sovereignty.

Kent's ascendancy was short-lived. The first major Anglo-Saxon kingdom was Northumbria, itself compounded of two smaller kingdoms, Bernicia and Deira. For fifty years from 600 onward, and especially under King Edwin, Northumbria asserted itself against the Britons of Strathclyde, the Picts of the North and the Scots of Argyll; it was formally converted to Christianity; it became the hive of the most remarkable achievements in art, literature and scholarship (for a fuller description, see pp. 105–113).

The so-called Golden Age of Northumbria (see page 100) lasted throughout the seventh century. But although Edwin was success-

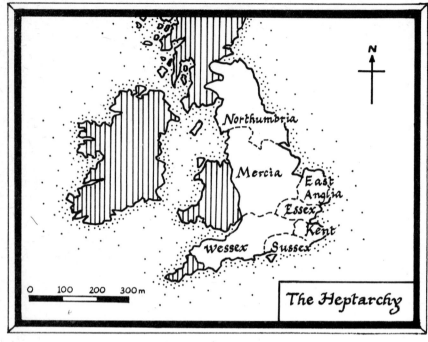

Map 2

ful in his forays to the north, he was undermined by the growing
power of Mercia and finally succumbed in 633 to the combined
armies of Penda of Mercia and Cadwallon of Wales. It was Penda
who first achieved the unity of Mercia, and from the death of
Edwin until almost the end of the seventh century the tide of
fortune ebbed and flowed between the Christian Northumbrians
and the heathen Mercians.

The burial ground of the Wuffingas, the royal house of the East
Angles, is at Sutton Hoo, near Woodbridge in Suffolk. Archaeologists investigated several of the bracken-covered mounds and,
as is so often the case, found that grave robbers had got there
first; but in 1939 one mound was discovered intact. Within it lay a
90-foot ship (see plate 12) of the seventh century and amidships
a rich funeral treasure (see colour plates 1, 2 and 3) – gold and
jewelled harness, a sceptre, a splendid shield, gold coins and a

sumptuous purse, buckets, cauldrons, ornamental iron chain work, shoes and combs, drinking horns, bottles, a lyre of maple wood and late Roman or Byzantine silver. These electrifying finds, perhaps the greatest archaeological discovery ever made in England, contribute immeasurably to our understanding of early European life and history: they prove, too, that even the subordinate kings (as the kings of East Anglia were to Mercia at this time) lived lives of a splendour previously thought to be unique to Northumbria. Most scholars believe *Beowulf* was composed in Northumbria at about this time. This poem, more than 3,000 lines long, is one of the most stirring works in our literature and it is the supreme statement of the heroic code; Beowulf himself, whose prodigious feats the poem describes, embodies loyalty and bravery and strives for *lof*, the fame that will survive a man's death. *Beowulf* is not a photograph, though; it is the work of a poet who was quite probably celebrating the glories of the past

12. The Sutton Hoo ship during re-excavation. It was first excavated in 1939. The iron rivets in the sides fastened the overlapping ship's timbers, which have now completely disintegrated.

as much as describing the realities of the present. Nevertheless, the discovery at Sutton Hoo not only endorses *Beowulf*'s picture of a well-endowed, sophisticated way of life but also makes it a distinct possibility that it is not Northumbrian but East Anglian in origin. Certainly the burial of East Anglian kings at Sutton Hoo cannot have been unlike this:

> Then the Geats built a barrow on the headland –
> it was high and broad, visible from far
> to all seafarers . . .
> They buried rings and brooches in the barrow,
> all those adornments that brave men
> had brought out from the hoard after Beowulf died.
> They bequeathed the gleaming gold, treasure of men,
> to the earth, and there it still remains,
> as useless to men as it was before.
> Then twelve brave warriors, sons of heroes,
> rode round the barrow, sorrowing . . .

Only one thing was missing from the mighty burial at Sutton Hoo: a body, or an urn full of ashes. *The Anglo-Saxon Chronicle* of 654 tells how Oswiu of Northumbria defeated and killed Penda of Mercia and Æthelhere of the East Angles at 'Winwædfeld'. And Bede has this to add:

> This battle was fought close to the River Winwæd, which at the time was swollen by heavy rains, and had flooded the surrounding country: as a result, many more were drowned while attempting to escape than perished by the sword.

So it is very possible that the mound at Sutton Hoo was a ceno-taph to Æthelhere whose body, like that of so many others, was swept away downstream and never recovered from the River Winwæd.

Thanks to Bede, we know a considerable amount about both the religious and political history of the seventh century. There is no corresponding record or set of annals to describe the way of life

of the band of warriors living in the basin of the upper Trent or
to explain how they so extended their power and influence that
Mercia became the most powerful kingdom in England throughout the later part of the seventh and the whole of the eighth
centuries. But this is what happened and, towards the end of the
eighth century, Offa emerges as the most powerful English king
before Alfred. He was a shrewd, ambitious and sometimes ruthless man. Where he could crush an opponent, he crushed him;
where he could not, he negotiated. During his reign he conquered Kent, ordered the beheading of one King of the East
Angles and became overlord of the whole of the south of England.

Offa maintained many links with the continent. He was the
only king whom Charlemagne treated as an equal. In fact Charlemagne called him 'his dearest brother' and unsuccessfully tried
to marry his son to Offa's daughter. Offa did, however, marry off
another of his daughters to the King of Wessex, to reduce any
threat from that quarter, the third great (and ultimately the
greatest) of the Anglo-Saxon kingdoms. One Anglo-Saxon word
for wife is 'freðu-webbe': peace-weaver.

Simply by virtue of his aggregated power in the south and
west, Offa exercised considerable influence in Northumbria. His
pugnacious face peers out at us from his coinage (see plate 32),
the finest in Europe at the time. He may not have been, as he
styled himself, *Rex totius Anglorum patriae*, but he was the next
best thing to it:

> King of the perennial holly-groves, the riven sandstone: overlord of
> the M5: architect of the historic rampart and ditch, the citadel at
> Tamworth, the summer hermitage in Holy Cross: guardian of the
> Welsh Bridge and the Iron Bridge: contractor of the desirable new
> estates: saltmaster: money-changer: commissioner for oaths: martyr-
> ologist: the friend of Charlemagne.
> 'I like that,' said Offa, 'sing it again.'*

Histories and Chronicles do not record the unspectacular. It is
true that in the seventh and eighth centuries the Anglo-Saxons

* Geoffrey Hill: *Mercian Hymns*, No. 1. André Deutsch, London, 1971.

often fought each other in the name of Christ or out of sheer ambition. But we are talking about eight generations. One does well to remember that the Anglo-Saxons probably talked no more and no less about the great political changes of their time than we talk about the disintegration of the Commonwealth, and Britain's attitude to the Common Market.

The Anglo-Saxon Chronicle itself is chiefly a record of alliance and counter-alliance, victory and defeat, the succession of kings, the consecration of bishops, pestilence and death. Sometimes an entry indicates how superstition-ridden the Anglo-Saxons were: 'In this year the star called the "comet" appeared; and Bishop Wilfrid was driven from his Bishopric by King Ecgfrith.' And again 'In this year there occurred in Britain bloody rain, and milk and butter were turned to blood.'

But the entry for the year 755 is altogether different. Far from being terse, it is a long, hectic account of how the King of Wessex and the brother of his predecessor fought, and were both killed, thereby playing into the hands of Offa who promptly secured greater control over Wessex. The strength of this entry, the first sustained piece of narrative prose in our language, resides in the attitudes of the warriors. After King Cyneheard has been discovered in the chamber of his mistress:

> ... they all fought against the king until they had slain him. Then by the woman's outcry, the king's thegns became aware of the disturbance and ran to the spot, each as he got ready and as quickly as possible. And the atheling made an offer to each of money and life; and not one of them would accept it. But they continued to fight until they all lay dead except for one British hostage, and he was severely wounded.

And again:

> Then they replied that no kinsman was dearer to them than their lord, and they would never serve his slayer.

This is a story of loyalty and treachery. One remembers Tacitus' words about Germanic warriors fighting for their leader, and their leader for victory; voices of the doomed men at Maldon; thanes at Hastings still fighting to avenge Harold knowing that the battle was already lost, and England with it.

The lord–retainer relationship was the cornerstone of Anglo-Saxon society. There was no greater virtue than loyalty; disloyalty led only to ruin and exile. The entry for 755 proclaims this truth, as well as giving us a glimpse of the rivalries and confusion of this period. The Anglo-Saxon poets reserve their greatest praise for loyalty; the serpentine patterning on the great gold buckle at Sutton Hoo (see colour plate 3) seems, among other things, to represent the way in which the fortunes of lord and retainer were inextricably meshed.

᠍᠍᠍᠍᠍

AGAINST THE VIKINGS

᠍᠍᠍᠍᠍

To the Anglo-Saxon, a dragon was half-real; he was the living embodiment of evil and, paradoxically, of death itself, a terrible scaly fire-breathing monster that any man might meet and heroes had met. The *Nibelungenlied* told how Sigurd (Wagner's Siegfried) had taken on and killed the dragon Fafnir; and the *Beowulf* poet related how the dragon 'flew in a flame-ball, burning for vengeance', and how it killed and was killed by Beowulf.

The dramatic entry in *The Anglo-Saxon Chronicle* for 793 reads:

> In this year dire portents appeared over Northumbria and sorely frightened the people. They consisted of immense whirlwinds and flashes of lightning, and fiery dragons were seen flying in the air. A great famine immediately followed those signs, and a little after that in the same year, on 8 June, the ravages of heathen men miserably destroyed God's church on Lindisfarne, with plunder and slaughter.

The 'heathen men' were of course the Vikings (see plate 13) making their first substantial, typically brutal, impact on Anglo-Saxon England. Over the sea they came in dragon-prows, marvellously elastic boats carrying 30 to 40 men, propelled by oar and sail, with elaborately carved prows decorated more often than not with a dragon's head and fanged jaws (see plate 14).

The word Viking, meaning 'bay-men' or 'fighting men' or 'settling men', refers collectively to the Danes, Norwegians and Swedes. Hungering for new land and suffering from overpopula-

13. Viking head carved from elk horn. 11th or 12th century.

14. Dragon stem post from the Oseberg ship.
9th century.

tion like the Germanic tribes in the fifth century, and often driven
abroad by political disunity that ended up as bloody feuding, the
Vikings thrust south, east and west as 'conquerors, discoverers,
merchants, and colonists.'*

Sailing south, the Vikings colonized parts of Great Britain,

* Gwyn Jones: *A History of the Vikings*.

France and Germany; some of them even settled in Sicily where there are reputedly still a few men and women with the fair skin and fair reddish hair of the Norsemen. Sailing east, the Vikings drove south through Russia from Novgorod to Kiev and so to the Black Sea, and Constantinople, where the Emperor's own guard consisted entirely of Vikings. At times humping their boats over land on pine rollers, the Vikings reached the River Volga too, and sailed south to the Caspian and thence as merchants to Baghdad, carrying with them 'sables, squirrel, ermine, black and white foxes, marten, beaver, arrows and swords, wax and birch-bark, fish-teeth and fish-lime, amber, honey, goatskins and horse-hides, hawks, acorns, hazel nuts, cattle and Slavonic slaves.'*
An Arab merchant and diarist, Ibn Fadlan, describes the Vikings as he saw them on the Volga in 922:

> I have seen the Rus as they came on their merchant journeys and encamped by the Atil (Itil, Volga). I have never seen more perfect human specimens, tall as date palms, blond and ruddy . . . Each man has an axe, a sword, and a knife, and keeps each by him at all times . . . Each woman wears on either breast a box of iron, silver, copper or gold; the value of the box indicates the wealth of the husband.

To the west the Vikings colonized first Iceland and then Greenland, which was only called 'Green' by its discoverer, Eric the Red, in order to entice others to follow him. From there, they sailed still farther west. That Leif Ericson reached Newfoundland and New England in the United States, and found 'fields of wild wheat growing there, and vines' is not mere speculation. The much-discussed Vinland Map showing Iceland, Greenland and a mainland farther to the west may well be a twentieth-century forgery, but recent archaeological excavations at L'Anse-aux-Meadows in Newfoundland have conclusively proved the existence of a Viking settlement there – some five centuries before Columbus set sail from Portugal and 'discovered' America.

The daring, sheer independence of spirit and strength of will

---

* Gwyn Jones: *A History of the Vikings.*

that prompted the Vikings to thrust so far in three different directions, is quite breathtaking. And wherever they went, they depended on navigational skill and superb ships – ships which are one of the great artistic and practical achievements of pre-Conquest Europe. Clinker-built (with iron rivets linking the overlapping planks) on a keel plank that swept up into a stem at either end, they were both beautiful in line (see plate 15) and very pliable in rough waters. They were propelled by oarsmen, perhaps 15 or 16 on each side in a fighting ship sitting in an enclosed deck, and by a square sail. The warriors' coloured shields hung in a row over the railings:

> I saw my two lords
> In Pentland Firth,
> A crossing of sword and axe.
> My sad songs are shrouds.
> Blood blotched the water,
> Blood quartered the gleaming shield,
> Blood stained stem-post and stern,
> Black blood oozed
> From the caulked seams.*

The Vikings could be gangsters as well as gangers. At times they were cruel and ruthless; they butchered defenceless monks; they raped women and slaughtered children; they could kill a man by drawing the blood-eagle on him – that is to say, slitting his backbone so that his ribs sprang apart, like wings, exposing the heart. Yet they have often been painted too black. Like the Anglo-Saxons, they were fatalists. They believed that 'humanity is born to trouble, but courage, adventure, and the wonders of life are matters for thankfulness, to be enjoyed while life is still granted to us'.† They maintained their own intense loyalties and values, and grasped voraciously at the possibility of winning a name that would live after them. They bring to ninth-century

---

* Translated by the author from the *Orkneyinga Saga*.
† H. Ellis Davidson: *Gods and Myths of Northern Europe*.

Europe an utterly distinctive dash, a sense of dangerous excitement.

15. The Gokstad ship. 9th century.

So in 793, out for gold and glory, Vikings sacked the monastery at Lindisfarne (see plate 16), the focal point of Christianity in the north of England. Alcuin spoke the words thousands must have felt:

> It is some 350 years that we and our forefathers have inhabited this lovely land, and never before in Britain has such a terror appeared as this we have now suffered at the hands of the heathen. Nor was it thought possible that such an inroad from the sea could be made.

But this was only a beginning. The Vikings sacked Jarrow the following year and the monastery of Iona in 795. Where at first a few came, doubtless astonished to find great hoards of gold undefended in monasteries so conveniently close to the sea, many followed. For seventy years Scotland and Ireland were subject to an increasing number of hit-and-run attacks from Norwegians; and summer after summer the Northumbrians were riddled with fear of black sails on the horizon and new boatloads of Danes. A line from the Anglo-Saxon litany reads:

> A furorum Normanorum, libera nos, Domine.
> (From the fury of the Norsemen, good lord deliver us.)

But in 865 there was a sinister shift of emphasis. *The Chronicle* notes:

> . . . a great heathen army came into England and took up winter quarters in East Anglia; and there they were supplied with horses, and the East Angles made peace with them.

This army was altogether different to the bands of raiders that preceded it. It was led by the sons of Ragnar Lothbrok, who were out to avenge their father: he had reputedly been thrown into a pit full of snakes and spoke the immortal last words: 'The piglets would be grunting if they knew the fate of the boar!' Ragnar's sons and their followers were ready to remain in England through the winter, even through several winters; from now on there was to be no seasonal respite from the Vikings.

The kingdom of Northumbria was the first to collapse, in 867.

16. Both sides of a 9th or 10th century tombstone from Lindisfarne:
Vikings on the rampage, monks at prayer.

The following year the Mercians bought off the Vikings with protection money, known as danegeld. After returning to East Anglia and encamping for the winter at Thetford, the Vikings fought the East Angles and savagely executed King Edmund early in 869. This confrontation of passive Christian king and wild heathen Vikings was remembered by generation after generation, and at the end of the tenth century it was celebrated by the great prose writer Ælfric, in his *Life of King Edmund*:

> And then the heathens became madly incensed because of his faith, for he always called Christ to his help. Then they shot at him with missiles, as if for their sport, until he was entirely surrounded by their shots, like the spikes of a hedgehog, as Sebastian was.

Ælfric tells how a grey wolf led Edmund's sorrowful followers to a copse where the Vikings had thrown his head, and how his head was miraculously rejoined to his body. Edmund's grave became the site of many miracles; and indeed Edmund later became the first of the three patron saints of England: he was succeeded by Edward the Confessor who was in turn replaced in the thirteenth century by St George, a Roman tribune martyred in Nicomedia to whom dragon-killing legends were later attached, and whose cult was brought to England from the East by returning Crusaders.

So in five years the 'micel here', or Great Army, had conquered Northumbria and East Anglia and brought Mercia to its knees. There was every reason to suppose that the country would soon succumb entirely. In 871 the Vikings moved again: 'In this year the army came into Wessex to Reading, and three days later two Danish earls rode further inland.'

It was the Vikings' misfortune to run at this time into one of the most remarkable men in world history, Alfred of Wessex, the one king the English have called Great. Alfred only succeeded to the throne by chance; the succession would normally have passed to his brother Ethelred's son, but he was only a young boy, and Wessex above all needed a battle-hardened leader. Alfred was that, as well as being loved and respected as a scholar, educationalist and lawmaker (see pp. 114–118). Now, in 870, his first

7. The Bayeux Tapestry. The Latin inscription reads in full LEVVINE ET GYRD FRATRES HAROLDI REGIS HIC CECIDVNT: Leofwine and Gyrth, the brothers of King Harold, have here fallen.

8. The Bayeux Tapestry. The Latin inscription reads in full HIC HAROLD REX INTERFECTUS EST: Here King Harold is killed.

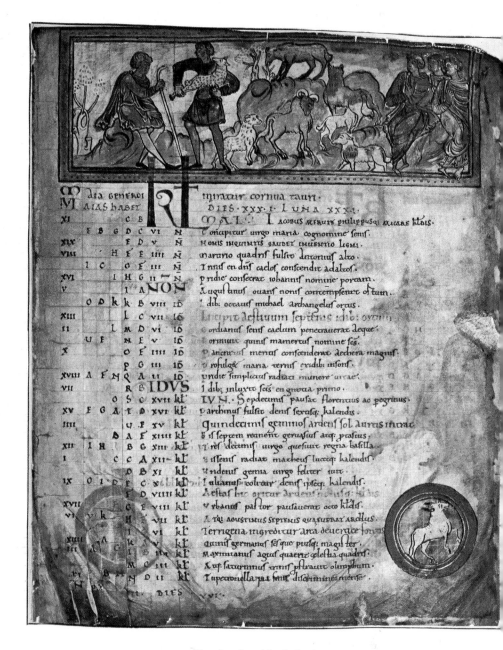

9. Shepherds with their sheep –
the illustration for May in an 11th-century calendar.

concern was to push the Vikings out of Wessex, and he rounded on them with such success that they settled for a truce at the end of that year. Alfred knew this respite would be temporary. At once he applied himself to coping with the unwillingness of the militia to remain in the field month after month, particularly during the spring and summer when the vital crops had to be sown and reaped. By the simple but bold expedient of halving his army, he ensured 'that there was always half at home and half on active service'; every three months, the two halves changed over. In one stroke, Alfred had ensured both agricultural continuity and continuity of action against the Vikings.

Alfred made other military innovations. He built fortresses throughout Wessex which could be used as refuges in time of need and, although it is an exaggeration to call him Father of the English Navy, he did build ships so as to harass the Vikings by sea as well as land.

For all this, the fate of Wessex hung long in the balance. At one point Alfred's fortunes were so low that he had to retreat beyond the forest of Selwood into Somerset and shelter in the marshes of Athelney. It was there that Alfred's jewel (see colour plate 4) was found. But the men of Somerset and Wiltshire and Hampshire rallied and in 878 the *Chronicle* reports the momentous victory of Alfred over the Vikings at Ethandune. The Vikings gave Alfred oaths that they would leave Wessex forthwith. This was a great milestone; it must have been the moment at which the Vikings, badly defeated for the first time, recognized that Alfred might always stand between them and the conquest of England. And some years later, in 886, Alfred (speaking for all free English people) and Guthrum (leader of the Danes) drew up a famous document, a treaty between two equal powers. It divided England into Wessex, including English Mercia, and Danelaw (see map 3) and forbade migration from one territory into the other. The document took account, moreover, of the status of English inhabitants living in Guthrum's kingdom and, by setting a high 'wergild' or mangold on their heads, entailed that there would be no discrimination against them.

This division of land was a realistic deal between realistic men.

Those who succeeded Alfred and Guthrum were less far-sighted and during the tenth century there was renewed fighting. At first the men of Wessex clawed back much lost land in the Midlands and East Anglia; but in 978 the succession of a twelve-year-old boy to the throne of Wessex coincided with the arrival from Denmark of new droves of 'wolvish Vikings, avid for slaughter'.

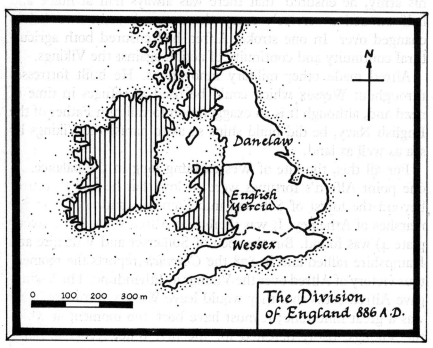

Map 3

The young King was Ethelred the Unready – a more accurate translation of *unræd* would be ill-advised. Ethelred was, for time and again he was counselled to buy peace, and time and again the Vikings returned for more. In one year alone 72,000 pounds of gold and silver were paid over in return for short-lived peace; no wonder so many Anglo-Saxon arm-bands, brooches, torques, ingots and coins have been unearthed by archaeologists in Scandinavia (see plate 17).

But listen to this voice:

> Can you hear, you pirate, what these people say?
> They will pay you a tribute of whistling spears,
> of deadly darts and proven swords,
> weapons to pay you, pierce, slit and slay you in
> storming battle . . .
> . . . over here there stands a noble earl with his
> troop –
> guardians of the people and of the country,
> the home of Ethelred, my prince – who'll defend
> this land
> to the last ditch.

The speaker is Byrhtnoth, who in 991 fought and was annihilated by one of the highly successful warbands that were ravaging England, at Maldon in Essex. What singles out this from other such encounters is that the battle was celebrated by an unknown poet who has given us a brilliant, horrifying picture of hand-to-hand fighting and of the extraordinary spirit that sustained the warriors.

At the start of a battle, the Anglo-Saxons formed a shield-wall: that is to say, they stood in a row, as many deep as possible, with overlapping shields. This was highly effective provided the enemy were not so many that they could burst through the wall or get round behind it. Later in the battle, many of the warriors fought in pairs – axeman and shield-bearer together, a fearsome combination. But at Maldon it was not enough; the poet introduces the sinister beasts of battle, waiting in the wings:

> The time had come
> for all the doomed men to fall in the fight.
> The clamour began; the ravens wheeled and the eagle
> circled overhead, craving for carrion; there was
> shouting on earth.

The poet bitterly condemns those who 'fled from the fight and saved their lives in the silent wood'. The punishment for cowardice

17. A silver treasure hoard found at Grimestad in Norway. 10th century.

was exile (see p. 85); discretion was not considered the better part of valour. If his lord had been killed, the lord's retainer had two alternatives: to avenge his lord by killing his enemies, or to lie slain beside him. After the death of Byrhtnoth, the doomed Anglo-Saxon warriors encourage one another. At the end, an old retainer, Byrhtwold, speaks. And his words sum up absolutely the Germanic heroic code which was just as real for the warriors at Maldon as for their ancestors who first sailed to this country:

> Mind must be the firmer, heart the more fierce,
> courage the greater, as our strength diminishes.
> Here lies our leader, dead,
> an heroic man in the dust.
> He who now longs to escape will lament for ever.
> I am old. I will not go from here,
> but I mean to lie by the side of my lord,
> lie in the dust with the man I loved so dearly.

Ethelred reigned from 978 until 1016: exhausting years for England at the end of which the country seemed as ripe for total conquest as it had done when Alfred came to the throne. But Ethelred's son Edmund Ironside and Canute, King of Norway and Denmark, struggled so inconclusively and destructively for the crown that they finally decided to divide the country between them; at this point Edmund Ironside, aged only 22, unexpectedly died and, sick of war, the English unanimously elected Canute king. England had become part of the kingdom of Scandinavia.

Canute ruled England well. He was remembered as a 'peace-bringer, legislator, administrator, statesman and politician, and as a patron of the Church'.* But when he died in 1035 his North Sea Empire collapsed and the English Crown eventually came to rest once more on an English head – that of Edward the Confessor (see p. 55 for a fuller description).

The last scene between Anglo-Saxons and Vikings was played out in 1066 when three men believed that they had a right to the throne of England: Harold Godwinson, who ruled the land for nine months; William the Bastard, Duke of Normandy; and Harald Hardrada of Norway, successor to part of the kingdom of

* Gwyn Jones: *A History of the Vikings.*

Canute. Hardrada, assisted by Harold Godwinson's own brother, Tostig – deposed in 1065 as Earl of Northumbria because of treachery – arrived in September in Yorkshire with 300 ships full of fighting men.

Harold of England, waiting anxiously for the expected arrival of William from Normandy, was taken by surprise. At once he marched north and on September 25th met the Norwegian army at Stamford Bridge on the River Derwent. *King Harald's Saga* records a remarkable meeting in which Harold Godwinson himself, in disguise, rode over to Tostig and Hardrada, saying that the King offered Tostig his Earldom back in return for peace. Tostig asked what Hardrada would be offered:

> The rider said, 'King Harold has already declared how much of England he is prepared to grant him: seven feet of ground, or as much more as he is taller than other men.'
> After the brothers had talked, Harold rode away:
> Then King Harald Sigurdsson asked, 'Who was that man who spoke so well?'
> 'That was King Harold Godwinsson,' replied Tostig.
> King Harald Sigurdsson said, 'I should have been told much sooner . . .'
> 'It is quite true, sire,' said Earl Tostig, 'that the king acted unwarily . . . (But) I would have been his murderer if I had revealed his identity. I would rather that he were my killer than I his.'

All day the two sides fought. Harald Hardrada was struck in the throat by an arrow, and fell dead under his famous banner, Land-Waster. Tostig was killed too. At the day's end, the Vikings had been mauled as never before on English soil; twenty-four ships were sufficient to carry the survivors back to Norway.

That was the end of the colourful, brutal, tangled and fascinating Viking Age in England. But the effort that finished off the Vikings had half-finished the Anglo-Saxons too. Three days after the Battle of Stamford Bridge William the Bastard arrived in England.

AGAINST THE NORMANS

THE question of who was the rightful successor to the throne after the death of Edward the Confessor has been argued for more than 900 years.

Edward's mother was Emma, daughter of a Duke of Normandy; and in his childhood and youth he had lived as an exile in Normandy for twenty-five years. So it was as natural as leaves to a tree that, when he became king (see plate 18), he should bring to Court many influential Normans. Indeed, it does seem likely that, at some stage, Edward (who had no son) actually promised the throne to Duke William of Normandy. On his death bed, however, Edward is said to have pointed at the most powerful thane in England, Harold Godwinson, and said, 'I commend my wife to your care, and with her my whole kingdom.'

Harold, and his father Godwine before him, was the mouthpiece of all those who resented the Normans at court as intruders.

18. Coin bearing the head of Edward the Confessor, 1042–1066.

Anxious to save England for the English, they now acclaimed him king; and on the same day that Edward the Confessor was buried in that great cathedral of his own devising, Westminster Abbey, Harold was crowned. This was no time for doubts or hesitations, though the comet 'which some call "the long-haired star"' (see plate 19), recorded in awe by the Anglo-Saxon Chronicler, later made people believe Harold would have done well to think twice. Comets have traditionally been seen as ill omens; that even applies to a limited extent to the recent Kohoutek.

But there is another witness: the Bayeux Tapestry. This brilliant strip cartoon, 230 feet long, and sewn in red and yellow and buff, blue and green, was embroidered in the south of England or in Normandy just after the Conquest; and in some seventy incidents (each with a Latin caption), full of suspense and teeming with movement and detail, it portrays the relation-

19. A section from the Bayeux Tapestry showing people pointing at 'the long-haired star'.

ship of William and Harold. Its masterly (though biased) story-teller begins with the arrival of Harold in 1063 at the Court of Guy, Duke of Ponthieu, who promptly takes him prisoner, and subsequently hands him over to Duke William; it depicts the friendship of William and Harold during the following year, in the course of which Harold bore arms for William against the Bretons; and it shows how Harold swore oaths of allegiance to William (see plate 20) perhaps undertaking to help him secure the English throne. That Harold swore some oath of this sort is certain. But did he do so voluntarily? And what would have happened if he had refused? He was, after all, a prisoner. These are the vital questions that cannot ever now be answered, and the background to William's arrival at Pevensey only three days after the Battle of Stamford Bridge.

20. The Bayeux Tapestry. In this scene, says the Latin caption, HAROLD SACRAMENTUM FECIT VVILLELMO DUCI: Harold made an oath to Duke William.

The timing could not have been worse for Harold. Yet, with a remarkable burst of energy and determination, he marched 190 miles back from York to London, and then a further 50 miles

south to Hastings, within 13 days. He could well have waited in
London both to regain energy after the arduous journey and for
further reinforcements. But Harold was impetuous and a man of
action; he was not a military strategist.

So at Hastings, throughout Saturday 14 October 1066, Anglo-
Saxons engaged Normans in the most crucial battle ever fought
in England. There were about 7,000 men on either side. The
Anglo-Saxon army consisted exclusively of infantry, relying on
the old and proven shield-wall; the Norman army consisted not
only of infantry but also of mounted knights and of archers. So
this was a battle between inflexible and flexible; thane and knight;
old and new.

For all that, the contest was very equal. No words describe the
action as well as the thrilling tumultuous scenes of the Bayeux
Tapestry, such as that in which Harold's two brothers are killed
(see colour plate 5) and the ghastly borders packed out with
lopped heads and lopped limbs, convulsed bodies pierced by
spear and arrow, warriors lying under their shields:

> Night was close now. English against Normans, Bretons, Frenchmen,
> one for all and all for one – the dying Harold or the bastard William.
> Man against man against man against man against man. One jack-
> knifed in agony; one marched on. Mace crushed helmet and head
> inside it, lance pierced mail-coat and heart behind it; one is one, all,
> alone, all, one . . .
> Spear and shriek and shield and shout and sword and scream and
> scream tore apart the silken evening air. Hands and horses, helmets,
> heads were trampled underfoot . . .*

The turning-point was undoubtedly the death of Harold. Only
later chroniclers (maybe misled by the position of the lettering)
suggested that Harold was struck in the eye by an arrow. In
colour plate 6 the figure on the right is almost certainly Harold,
cut down as the hill he had so long defended under his banner,

* From 'The Eye of the Hurricane' by the author in *Wordhoard* by Jill Paton
Walsh and Kevin Crossley-Holland.

The Fighting Man, was overwhelmed by Normans on horseback, supported by their archers.

William won a great battle but, as he feasted by flaming torch-light amongst the corpses, he must still have anticipated further resistance. Some towns quickly and prudently surrendered:

21. The forbidding Norman keep of Dover Castle. 11th century.

Dover, Canterbury, Winchester and then, most significantly, London. But William was never able to pin down one dissident, Edric the Wild who, assisted by Welsh princes (descendants of those the Anglo-Saxons had themselves fought so long before) created great trouble in Mercia; he was so concerned and angered by the Northumbrian uprisings of 1068 and 1069 that, after the city of York had been sacked by a combined force of Northumbrians and Danes, he ravaged much of the north in 1069 and in 1070 in a systematic and brutal attempt to destroy the means of life in northern England; and in 1070 William was troubled further by Hereward, a Lincolnshire thane who used the Isle of Ely as a base, was assisted like the Northumbrians by Danish seamen, sacked Norman Peterborough and proved as elusive as the marsh mists. It was five years after Hastings before William had firm and final control (see plate 21) over the entire country.

To us now, the victory of the Normans seems inevitable. It was a success for crude, violent, grasping, efficient systematizers, the logical outcome of organized ambition. And it was, of course, a decisive step towards the future medieval world that Richard Barber explores in *A Strong Land and a Sturdy*.* But to the Anglo-Saxon Chronicler writing in 1067, describing what happened when William the Conqueror returned overwinter to Normandy, things could barely have seemed more bleak:

> And Bishop Odo and Earl William stayed behind and built castles far and wide throughout the country, and distressed the wretched folk, and always after that it grew much worse. May the end be good when God wills!

---

* Richard Barber: *A Strong Land and a Sturdy*. Mirror of Britain Series, André Deutsch, London, 1976.

DAILY LIFE

THE THANE

THE well-born Anglo-Saxon layman had an ambition he could put a name to. He wanted to win fame for courage, loyalty, and dignity in the teeth of implacable fate. An Old Norse proverb goes, 'One thing I know never dies nor changes, the reputation of a dead man.' Anglo-Saxons would have said the same. The final word of *Beowulf* is 'lofgeornost', most eager for fame.

At the heart of the code by which the Anglo-Saxons lived lay the crucial relationship between a thane and his retainers or followers. As Tacitus noted, and as exemplified by the followers of Cyneheard (see p. 38) and of Byrhtnoth at Maldon (see p. 52), the axis of this relationship was absolute loyalty.

A retainer volunteered military service in time of war, and in peacetime various agricultural services – such as working on his lord's land for a day or more each week, and giving him produce. In return, the thane gave his retainer horses and weapons (known as heriot, or war-gear); from time to time he gave him treasure and feasted him; he gave him a gold ring (see plate 22) as a symbol of their attachment; and, above all, he gave protection. In *The Beginnings of English Society*, Dorothy Whitelock says: 'The relationship of lord and follower involved the duty of vengeance by the survivor if either were slain – or, at the very least, the exaction of a compensation high enough to do honour to the slain man.' Vengeance was also the duty of a slain man's kindred; to them the 'wergild' or man-gold was payable, and it was fear of precipitating a vendetta that acted as one force for law and order in Anglo-Saxon England.

22. Gold ring. The inscription reads, æDREDMECAHEAnREDM
ECagROF: Ædred owns me, Eanred engraved me. 9th century.

Kinship and romantic love meant much to the Anglo-Saxons
as we shall see, but probably neither meant quite as much as a
well-founded relationship between a thane and his retainer.
Listen to this lament of a man who has lost his lord:

> He remembers hall-retainers and how in his youth
> he had taken treasure from the hands of his gold-friend
> after the feast. Those joys have all vanished.
> A man who lacks advice for a long while
> from his lord and friend lives thus in his loneliness:
> in restless sleep he dreams that he clasps
> and kisses his lord, and lays hands and head
> upon his lord's knee, just as he had done
> when he approached the gift-throne previously.
> Then the lonely wanderer wakes again
> and sees the dark waves surging around him,
> the sea-birds bathing and spreading their feathers,
> snow flakes falling mingled with hail.

This is the love poetry of a heroic society; one can find similar
passages in the *Iliad* and the *Odyssey*. We are talking about a time
when survival seemed still a day-to-day matter and weapons lay
at a man's bedside; the chief bond was of man for man, not of
man for woman.

A thane was a thane because he owned (usually through inherit-
ance) at least five hides of land – that is, approximately one
square mile. The way in which the law recognized a thane was
by his value in 'wergild'. In some parts of the country, a thane
was referred to as a man 'of twelve hundred' because he was
worth 1,200 shillings; this was between three and six times as
much as the churl or small farmer.

After the departure of the Romans, the art of building in stone
was largely forgotten; an eighth-century poet, looking in awe at
the ruins of Roman municipal buildings, refers to them as 'the
work of giants'. Most Anglo-Saxon houses were built of wood.

The thane lived in a 'burh' or home fortified by a surrounding
earthwork and stockade. Its focal point was the single-storied
hall, anything up to 100 feet in length (see plate 23). The *Beowulf*-
poet speaks admiringly of the hall Heorot as 'lofty and wide-
gabled'; he describes the tapestries hanging on the walls and the
long trestle tables and the mead-benches 'studded with gold'. In a
place such as this, the day's business would be done and, after

23. Reconstruction of an Anglo-Saxon hall at West Stow in Suffolk.

dark, the place was given over to pastimes and feasting. Overnight, many retainers might sleep in the hall: 'Benches were pushed back,' says the *Beowulf*-poet, 'the floor was padded with beds and pillows.'

Leading off the hall, there were separate small huts where the thane, his family and guests slept and where foodstuffs and tools were stored. Gone were the graceful villas of the Romans; the elegant mosaics and elaborate bath-houses had given way to something altogether more rudimentary.

Anglo-Saxon poetry tells us much about the thane in time of war; it is the laws that best indicate his peacetime duties: he had to attend the king's court, appear at legal assemblies, maintain law and order in his own area, and keep local bridges in good repair. For some, there were such occasional duties as riding in pursuit of cattle-raiders, fitting out a new ship, 'the building of deer-hedges on the king's estate', or, like one man in *Beowulf*, acting as a coastguard:

> Then Hrothgar's thane leaped onto his horse
> and, brandishing a spear, galloped
> down to the shore; there, he asked at once:
> 'Warriors! Who are you, in your coats of mail,
> who have steered your tall ships over the sea-lanes
> to these shores?'

In addition to his public duties, the thane must have been much preoccupied with the management of his own land and the arrangements with the many small farmers who leased land from him, worked for him, and paid him with produce; the thane was in effect Chaucer's knight and reeve rolled into one. Many thanes owned more than one estate and we know, for example, that after Byrhtnoth's death at Maldon, his widow sold off no less than thirty-six estates.

The first preoccupation of the thane's wife was the rearing of her family (see plate 24) and the supervision of the household. This must have been no light matter, for like a modern kibbutz the 'burh' was virtually self-sufficient. It provided its own meat: animals were fattened and slaughtered and, before winter, salted.

24. Detail from the *Benedictional of St Æthelwold*. Late 10th century.

It grew its own vegetables. And it baked its own bread:

> I'm told a certain object grew
> in the corner, rose and expanded, threw up
> a crust. A proud wife carried off
> that boneless wonder, the daughter of a king
> covered that swollen thing with a cloth.

The Anglo-Saxons had a great thirst on them, though not as great as that of the Norse god Thor who is said to have been tricked into drinking half the ocean through a bottomless horn (see plate 25). A thane's wife had to oversee the brewing of ale, and of mead which was made then, as it is today, from fermented honey, which were kept in rather soft black and grey-brown pottery urns. Honey was the only form of sweetening known to the Anglo-Saxons and consequently great importance was attached to bees and bee-keeping. A charm survives, words once spoken to restrain bees:

When they swarm, scatter earth over them and say:
'Alight, victorious women, alight on the earth!
Never turn wild and fly to the woods!
Be just as mindful of *my* benefit
as is every man of his food and his fatherland.

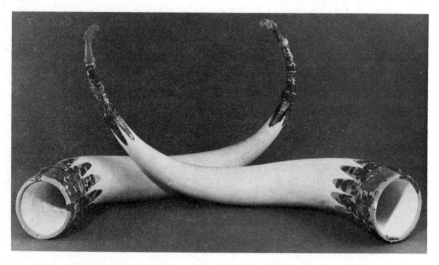

25. Reconstructions of drinking horns; the ornamental silverwork was found in the Sutton Hoo ship-burial. 7th century. The Anglo-Saxons used the horns of the cow and of the auroch, the extinct wild ox of Northern Europe. These horns each have a capacity of six quarts.

Apart from the provision of food and drink, a thane's wife also supervised the weaving and dyeing of clothes for her family and followers. This would have entailed the combing and carding and spinning of wool, and then the work of weaving itself, the rattle of the shuttle and the bang of the weaver's rod, and the threads thrashing in the thrumming loom. There is plenty of evidence that the Anglo-Saxons cared about their appearance. Men wore knee-length tunics and trousers, and a mantle – usually wool but sometimes fur; women wore tunics and full-length kirtles; and both sexes used jewellery, rings and armlets and necklets, brooches and buckles. Anglo-Saxon jewellery used two techniques, chip-carving and polychrome jewelling. In the former (see plate 26), a piece of metal was incised with animal ornaments and abstract linear shapes, and occasionally with human figures. The same forms – which were also used in manuscript illumination – occur in polychrome work (see colour plate 2), where a base plate of gold is covered with gold or silver cells inlaid with garnets, coloured glass, niello (a black metallic alloy) and cowrie shells. The finest Anglo-Saxon jewellery is technically as brilliant as anything made before or since, and artistically a delight.

The thane's wife had a public as well as a private persona. She was mistress of ceremonies in the feasting-hall. And when she

26. The Fuller Brooch. Made of silver inlaid with niello, it illustrates the five senses: taste (top left), hearing (bottom left), smell (top right), touch (bottom right) and sight (in the middle). 9th century.

offered advice, she was listened to. In *Beowulf*, the Queen Wealh-theow anticipates problems over the succession and shrewdly tells her husband:

> I am told you intend to adopt this warrior,
> take him for your son . . .
>
> . . . give many rewards
> while you may, but leave this land and the Danish people
> to your own descendants when the day comes
> for you to die.

The thane's wife also had rights quite independent of her husband. She could own land, defend herself in the courts, have slaves and set them free at her own discretion, and inherit money and use it as she wanted. These things may seem ordinary enough; they seem extraordinary when compared to the sub-servient role to which women were relegated for many centuries after the Norman Conquest.

Life was not all work. The thane was a keen huntsman (see

27. Huntsmen with spears. A detail from the *Cædmon Genesis*. c. 1000.

plate 27) of both fox and 'moor-stalker, the stag with strong horns'. He kept a hawk;

> One will tame that arrogant wild bird,
> the hawk on the fist, until the falcon
> becomes gentle; he puts jesses on it
> and feeds it still in fetters; he weakens
> the swift peregrine, so proud of its plumage,
> with mere morsels until that bird, servile
> in garment and in flight, obeys its sustainer,
> is trained to the hand of the young warrior.*

The thane tested his horses, and enjoyed bull-baiting and cock-fighting. And then there were indoor pastimes too: a few men (more as time went on) were literate enough to read and rich enough to possess one or two manuscripts. Draughts and dicing were played, and so too was chess (see plate 28).

But it is quite clear from innumerable references in Old English poetry that the thane enjoyed nothing so much as the cameraderie of his friends and followers, and the songs of the storytelling poet, in the mead hall. One has to imagine a sudden long darkness, especially in winter, held at bay only by the soft light of candles. What was there to do? Very little but talk and eat and drink, or else go to bed. So it is that the feast came to enjoy a special significance: there the thane and his followers made boasts which were a kind of bet based on self-knowledge. Each man estimated his ability, and his friends remembered it, and later commented on how he had realized or fallen short of his estimate. So, at Maldon the poet comments:

> Offa was quickly brought down in the battle.
> Yet he had kept his promise to his prince;
> he fulfilled his former boast to Byrhtnoth, the ring-giver,
> that they should either return unhurt, riding to the stronghold
> in victory together, or together surrender their lives,
> bleeding from wounds on the battlefield.

> * Lines from 'The Fates of Men'.

28. Viking chessmen found on the Isle of Lewis in the Hebrides.
12th century.

It is impossible to think long about the Anglo-Saxons without thinking of the feasting-hall. It was a place of clamour and ceremony:

    Dejected, I journeyed far and wide
hunting for the hall of a generous gold-giver,
for a man who would welcome me into his mead-hall,
give me good cheer (for I boasted no friends),
entertain me with delights. He who has experienced it
knows what a cruel companion sorrow can be
to any man who has few loyal friends.*

In the feasting-hall the thane and his wife sat together with the specialist workmen, the sower and oxherd, cowherd and shepherd, the falconer and forester, the huntsman and the dog-keeper, the blacksmith, carpenter, tailor, salter, baker, cook, sempstress, weaver, and in one corner the luckless slaves, all of them silent, listening to the poet (see p. 91) warn them that

    Nothing is ever easy in the kingdom of earth,
the world beneath the heavens is in the hands of fate

and tell them once more that

    Each man should strive, before he leaves
this world, to win the praise of those living after him.

* Lines from 'The Wanderer'.

᭤᭤᭤᭤᭤᭤

THE SMALL FARMER

᭤᭤᭤᭤᭤᭤

THE Anglo-Saxons changed the way England looked. They came to a country of moor, heath and marsh but, above all, a country covered with vast forests of oak, ash and beech. To some it must have seemed a forbidding place:

> My husband's kinsmen force me to live in a forest grove,
> under an oak tree in this earth-cave.
> This cavern is age-old; I am choked with longings.
> Gloomy are the valleys, too high the hills,
> harsh strongholds overgrown with briars,
> joyless wasteland.*

Lines like these would have intoxicated those Romantic painters at the beginning of the nineteenth century who were inspired by precipitous rock, contorted tree trunk and tumult of water. But for the Anglo-Saxons, the forests penetrable only along the Roman roads and ancient trackways were not a curiosity to visit but a reality to live with:

> . . . a wondrously wild wood in a valley
> With high hills on each side overpeering a forest
> Of huge heavy oaks, a hundred together.
> The hazel and the hawthorn were intertwined,
> And all was overgrown with hoar-frosted moss,

* Lines from 'The Wife's Lament'.

And on the bleak branches birds in misery
Piteously piped away, pinched with cold.*

To make room for themselves, the Anglo-Saxons began to clear the woodlands. In some places they used that most devastating weapon, fire: in Essex, for instance, Brentwood means Burnt Wood. But for the most part it was slow demanding work with axe and billhook:

> Strong are the roots of the briars,
> So that my arms are broken
> Working at them again and again.†

In the forest clearings, first opened up by fire or by axe, and maintained by the grazing of animals, the Anglo-Saxons built their homes. What archaeological remains there are suggest that the house of the small farmer was far from luxurious. More often than not it consisted simply of one room where the family met, talked, ate and slept. The walls were made either of wood, or of lath and plaster; the roof was often thatched and had a hole in the middle which served as a chimney – the fire burned in an open hearth in the middle of the room. One of the paradoxes of Anglo-Saxon society is that people living in semi-squalor should have produced such sophisticated works of art.

Anglo-Saxon settlements were of two kinds: nuclear and linear. At the centre of a nuclear settlement was a green and, usually, a well (and, later, a church). Remains of an Anglo-Saxon village built round a well have been unearthed within the imposing walls of the Roman shore fort at Portchester; plate 29 shows how the Anglo-Saxons constructed a rectangular well within the earlier circular Roman pit, made of vertical planks cross-strutted with horizontal braces, carefully pegged together.

---

* From *Sir Gawain and the Green Knight*. These lines were written in the 14th century, but seem appropriate.
† Lines from an ancient Cornish drama, *The Creation of the World*.

29. Anglo-Saxon well within the walls of Portchester Castle, Hampshire

W. G. Hoskins writes:

It seems likely that these villages built around the perimeter of a large green or a square represent enclosures for defensive purposes, like the native villages of some East African tribes today. Here the huts are grouped around the perimeter of a circular pound . . . Into these pounds the livestock are driven at night for fear of the lions. In the villages of Saxon England, the necessity for protection from wolves in forested country may well have led to the same plan being adopted . . .*

★ W. G. Hoskins: *The Making of the English Landscape.*

The linear settlement was strung out along a single road. This heartless kind of village probably occurred when settlers made use of an existing road, rather than going to the trouble of making a new one. As one travels through England today, it is easy enough to pick out nuclear and linear villages. The great majority are Anglo-Saxon or Viking in origin, many of the former ending in -burgh or -borough, many of the latter in -by or -thorpe. Very few villages on the map today do not appear in William the Conqueror's Domesday Book. It was in the time of the Anglo-Saxons that this country first became a land of little villages and clear spaces.

Surrounding each village, whether nuclear, linear, or simply a scatter of homes where one had settled and others followed, lay either two or three vast open fields. These fields were divided into strips of between 1/3 and 1/2 an acre; that is, about half the size of a football pitch. Some kind of boundary marker, often a boulder, demarcated one strip from the next; it was only in the Middle Ages, and in Tudor times, that these great open fields came to be divided by hedges. But even now, an aerial photograph (plate 30) can hint at how these great fields, divided into strips, must have looked.

The strips were shared amongst the villagers, 'and an individual holder did not receive adjacent strips, but scattered over the fields as they fell to him by rotation.'* This was to ensure a fair deal: every villager had his share of fertile and less fertile land, nearby and distant land.

Different villagers were entitled to a different number of strips. The best off was the churl. In contrast with his lord, the thane, who had to own at least five hides of land, the churl owned at least one hide: that is, something between 60 and 120 acres – a holding that compares very reasonably with a small farmholding today. The churl was a freeman. He was entitled to attend popular assemblies; he was not bound to the soil. He could leave his land to his sons and there are instances of churls acquiring sufficient land to achieve the status of thane.

* W. G. Hoskins: *The Making of the English Landscape.*

30. Ridge and furrow at Crimscote, Warwickshire.

Less well off were the gebur and cotsetlan who rented their homes and land from their lord. Conditions varied from place to place, but on average the gebur worked 20 acres and the cotsetlan a meagre 5 or 6 acres. Many were further bound to their lord by extensive agricultural service: they tendered to him money, barley, hens and a sheep at different times of the year; and they worked two days each week and three days at harvest time on his land. In Ælfric's *Colloquy* (a dialogue used in the monastery schools to teach Latin), the ploughman says:

> *Ploughman*: O Master, I work very hard; I go out at dawn, drive the oxen to the field, and yoke them to the plough. There is no storm so severe that I dare to hide at home, for fear of my lord, but when the oxen are yoked, and the share and coulter have been fastened to the plough, I must plough a whole acre or more every day.
>
> *Teacher*: Have you any companion?
>
> *Ploughman*: I have a boy to urge on the oxen with a goad; he is now hoarse on account of the cold and his shouting.
>
> *Teacher*: What else do you do during the day?
>
> *Ploughman*: I do a great deal more. I must fill the bins of the oxen with the hay, water them, and carry off their dung.
>
> *Teacher*: Oh! Oh! the labour must be great!
>
> *Ploughman*: It is indeed great drudgery, because I am not free.

Technically the gebur and cotsetlan *were* freemen, but in practice they were yoked to their lord like oxen to the plough (see plate 31). Unlike the churl, they did not have the incentive of ownership; when they died, their homes and possessions and land had to be given over to their lord. As the centuries passed, it seems that the strong became stronger and the weak weaker. Thanes gave churls, geburs, and cotsetlan protection in restless times, but they made them pay heavily for it.

The most important animal to the Anglo-Saxon farmer was the sheep (see colour plate 7) for its wool, some of which was exported, milk and, of course, meat. In Ælfric's *Colloquy*, the teacher asks: 'What have you to say, shepherd? Have you any work?'

31. Men ploughing with oxen – the illustration for January in an
11th-century calendar.

Shepherd: Indeed I have. In the early morning I drive my sheep to
their pasture, and in heat and cold I stand over them with dogs,
lest wolves devour them. And I lead them back to their folds, and
milk them twice a day; besides this, I move their folds, and make
cheese and butter, and I am faithful to my lord . . .

The small farmer also raised cattle, pigs and goats. And in the
open fields he grew above all barley, which was used for making
bread and from which malt was extracted for brewing; oats and
wheat; flax for cloth-making; and woad for dyeing. The most
common vegetables were rye, beans and peas.

Both before and after they migrated to England, the great
majority of Anglo-Saxons were an agricultural people. Old
English poetry is not much concerned with the ordinary and it is
only through the riddles, Ælfric's charming *Colloquy*, illustra-
tions in a calendar, decorations on a font, that we are given a
picture of workaday life in England 1,000 years ago. What we
can discern is a people just about making do, but as vulnerable as

Indians or Ethiopians today to a disastrous harvest. 'In this year the great famine occurred in England' notes *The Chronicle* for 976, and we can only guess at how many perished because of it. We get a picture of men with their noses to the soil. And yet, although the Anglo-Saxons had very little of the mysterious imagination of their Celtic neighbours, we do also get a picture of the Anglo-Saxons marvelling at the wonderful strangeness of things – natural phenomena, animal and bird life, manmade objects: a bookworm gorging words it cannot understand, a pair of bellows with its stomach sticking out behind it, a ship with ribs but no shoulders or arms or hands, the moon stealing light from the sun. Poets made people look at the old with new eyes. The riddle 'Creation' begins:

> I stretch beyond the bounds of the world,
> I'm smaller than a worm, outstrip the sun,
> I shine more brightly than the moon. The swelling of the seas,
> the fair face of the earth and all the green fields,
> are within my clasp.

Nothing sums up the round of the small farmer's life better than the panels on the eleventh century font in Burnham Deepdale church in Norfolk (see plate 32). The seasons turn: in January a man sits with a drinking horn, and in February he warms himself at a fire; in March he digs with his spade and in

32. The 11th-century font in the church at Burnham Deepdale in Norfolk.
Read the months from right to left.

April he prunes; May he 'beats the bounds' with a banner; he weeds in June and scythes in July; in August he binds a sheaf; September he threshes with a flail, and grinds corn in a quern in October; November he slaughters a pig; and in December he feasts with his friends.

CODICIBVS SACRIS HOSTILI CLADE PERVSTIS
ESDRA DO FERVENS HOC REPARAVIT OPVS

10. An illustration from the *Codex Amiatinus* showing
the scribe Ezra with his books. Early 8th century.

11. Portrait of St Matthew in the *Book of Durrow*.
7th century.

TOWN, TRADESMAN AND TRAVELLER

᠗᠗᠗᠗᠗᠗

T HE Roman towns scattered through England were little capitals; they were centres of military activity, and trade and local government. Anglo-Saxon society, which revolved around the king's court and the thane's 'burh', had no immediate use for the impressive Roman municipal buildings; for perhaps a couple of centuries they were largely ignored:

> Their deserted ramparts became waste places,
> the derelict city decayed. Its warriors and craftsmen
> lie dead in the earth . . .
> > > . . . The ruins have tumbled to the plain,
> broken into craggy mounds of stone.*

Under pressure from the Danes, King Alfred fortified no fewer than thirty-one Wessex towns, but it was mainly the development of trade that led to the partial resettlement of many Roman towns. In all probability each townsman had his own strip of land in or outside the walls and shared grazing rights on the common (or commonly held) land. One is reminded of Woodhouse Moor in Leeds, part of it grassed and part of it divided into allotments where the townsmen cultivated vegetables during World War II and have done ever since. The Anglo-Saxons resorted to the Roman towns simply because they were situated in the most useful places – at the crossing of roads, beside navigable rivers,

* Lines from 'The Ruin'.

or by the sea. They also erected towns on new sites: Oxford, for instance, and Wallingford.

Seventy-one boroughs or towns are mentioned in the Domesday Book. The most important seem to have been London, York and Winchester, Lincoln, Chester, Canterbury, Oxford, Hereford, Thetford, Gloucester, Worcester, Norwich and Ipswich. London and York became two links in an extraordinary trade chain that extended not only throughout Europe but into the Middle East, Asia and North Africa. The Sutton Hoo ship-burial reflects this network: it contains, for instance, a vast silver dish bearing two control stamps of the Byzantine Emperor Anastasius I; a bronze bowl decorated with a donkey and a lion and another feline, probably made in Egypt; and thousands of garnets brought from India along land and sea trade routes to the workshop of some East Anglian jeweller. The merchants were predominantly Frisians, Jews and Arabs. In *The Anglo-Saxons*, D. M. Wilson writes:

> The Frisians . . . were a maritime people who had colonies in London and York and travelled between the great Baltic ports of the Viking Age, Birka, Haithabu and Schiringshal, carrying thither Rhenish wine, English and Frankish weapons, hunting dogs, oriental silks and English cloth, to barter for ropes, amber, furs – fox, beaver, sable and ermine – and slaves.

Naturally enough, Frisian merchants sometimes married Anglo-Saxon girls. Lines from the 'Gnomic Verses' tell how

> Dear is the welcome one
> to the Frisian wife when the ship sails in;
> his boat is berthed, her own husband is back,
> the man who maintains her, and she leads him home.
> She washes his salt-stained garments and gives him
> clean clothing;
> She grants him on land all that he, her lover, asks.
> A wife must observe her marriage oath; women are
> often deceivers.

This poem promulgates the reverse of the usual idea that a sailor has a girl in every port. But women deceived their husbands at their own peril; the punishment was cruel. One of Canute's laws reads:

> If a woman during her husband's lifetime commits adultery with another man, and it becomes known, let her afterwards become herself a public disgrace and her lawful husband is to have all that she owns, and she is to lose her nose and ears.*

Not only Frisians but Anglo-Saxons were merchants too. The dialogue in Ælfric's *Colloquy* gives some idea both of the hardship of the merchant's life and of the luxuries he was importing into the country:

> *Merchant*: I go aboard my ship with my wares, and row over parts of the sea, selling my goods, and buying precious things which cannot be produced in this country. Then with great peril on the sea, I bring them here to you. Sometimes I suffer shipwreck, and lose all my things, scarce escaping with my life.
> *Teacher*: What things do you bring us?
> *Merchant*: Purple garments and silks; precious gems and gold; strange raiment and spice; wine and oil; ivory and brass; copper and tin; sulphur and glass, and many such things . . .

The riddle 'Storm' describes the hazards of seafaring too, when 'a cargo of souls' rides foaming 'on the spines of breakers'. No wonder, then, that a man who had crossed the sea three times at his own risk was entitled to become a thane. Thanes depended on merchants for luxuries; monks depended on merchants for rare dyes with which they illuminated their manuscripts; and kings not only drank imported Rhenish wine and wore ermine but welcomed news of the arrival of each shipload – for as time passed, they appreciated that stiff trade regulations and taxes and tolls could be an entirely dependable source of royal revenue.

The king had absolute control over the amount of coinage

* *English Historical Documents, Volume I.*

actually available in his kingdom. Almost every borough seems
to have had its own mint, and new dies were constantly being
cast in an attempt to prevent forgery. There was, however, little
coinage in circulation by comparison with the present day because
so much was paid for with goods and service. Even so, no less
than 100,000 Anglo-Saxon silver pennies minted between 975
and 1050 have been found in Scandinavia, Danegeld carted home
by extortionate Viking warriors. The finest of the Anglo-Saxon
coins (see plate 33) are beautifully wrought. In *Anglo-Saxon
Pennies*, Michael Dolley writes:

> The general standard of Offa's coinage is remarkably high, artistic-
> ally as well as technically, and it is noteworthy that his pennies which
> have been found quite widely on the Continent were admired there
> sufficiently for their types to be imitated at Lucca on the road to
> Rome.

33. Coin bearing
the head of Offa,
757–796.

The Roman roads used by the merchants to travel their wares
and carry them to king's court and thane's burh, must have been
pitted and rutted, thick with weeds in summer and mud in
winter; still, they were as good as any country road in England
up to the end of the nineteenth century. A detail from the Bayeux
Tapestry gives some idea of the carts (plate 34) that jolted along
them.

In Anglo-Saxon England people only travelled if they had to:
there was little of the medieval jostle, the great pilgrimages to

34. Illustration of a cart in the Bayeux Tapestry.

Walsingham and Canterbury. But of course there was a certain amount of coming and going: not only merchants and foreign emissaries but ealdormen and thanes on their way to or back from court; and pedlars carrying countless wares (see plate 35) and iron 'to be made into ploughshares, fishooks, and tools of all kinds by local smiths',* and distributing salt from the coveted saltpans at Droitwich, and elsewhere for the winter preservation of meat. There would have been monks on the road too, moving from settlement to settlement, carrying the new faith, converting and comforting. And, least to be envied, there was the occasional luckless exile.

There were many ways in which a retainer might become, voluntarily or involuntarily, an exile; he could betray his lord (as Godwine and Godwig betrayed Byrhtnoth at Maldon), or fail to avenge him in battle; or his lord might die a natural death and have no successor. Similarly, a man might be separated from his wife or loved one, perhaps because of a feud. The lot of the exile, deprived of land and out on the road in search of another lord, has given rise to some of the finest Old English poetry – lines which convey brilliantly through descriptions of personal

* Dorothy Whitelock: *The Beginnings of English Society*.

35. A 10th-century comb cut from walrus ivory.

loss a sense of universal loss: friends dying, buildings collapsing, time passing. So it is that 'the Wanderer' says:

> . . . He who has experienced it
> knows what a cruel companion sorrow can be
> to any man who has few loyal friends.
> For him are the ways of exile, in no wise twisted gold!
> For him is a frozen body, in no wise the fruits of the earth!
> He remembers hall-retainers and how in his youth
> he had taken treasure from the hands of his gold-friend
> after the feast. Those joys have all vanished.

The Wanderer becomes more passionate and yet more stoical as he broods on the lost joys of the mead hall, the death of his warrior band, and at last he asks in words which seem to question the whole meaning of life:

> Where has the horse gone? Where the man? Where the
> > giver of gold?
> Where is the feasting-place? And where the pleasures
> > of the hall?
> I mourn the gleaming cup, the warrior in his corslet,
> the glory of the prince. How time has passed away,
> darkened under the shadow of the night even as if it
> > had never been.

It is true that the Anglo-Saxons relished their sense of melancholy, but as one reads the poems known as the elegies, one is struck again and again by the accumulating images of loss and loneliness underneath that melancholy: in 'The Wanderer' a man whose lord has died; in 'The Wife's Lament' and 'Wulf', both poems of true romantic love, a woman separated from her husband by a family feud, and a mistress calling out for her lover. For all of them, and for any pagan Anglo-Saxon exile, there was no comfortable answer:

> Worldly possessions are ephemeral, friends pass away,
> the whole world becomes a wilderness.

॥॥॥॥॥॥

AT COURT

॥॥॥॥॥॥

'I am Sigeferth,' shouts one of the heroes of 'The Finnesburh Fragment':

> . . . a warrior of the Secgan
> and a well-known campaigner. I've survived
> many conflicts, many stern trials. Here, in strife with me,
> you'll discover your fate, victory or defeat.

Wherever we look in Anglo-Saxon poetry, a man is no sooner mentioned than 'placed': 'Onela the son of Ongentheow', for example, or 'Godric the son of Æthelgar'. Many British surnames originated in the same way – in England, Jacobson, Smithson, Johnson and all those names ending in -son; in Scotland and Ireland all those names beginning with Mac- or Mc- (meaning 'son of') such as McLeod, MacBeth, McIlwraith, Macauley; and in Wales names such as Pugh and Price which derive from ap Huh (that is, 'son of Hugh') and ap Rhys.

Anglo-Saxon kings, following the extravagant example of the Old Testament, were quick to ensure that annalists recorded and poets sang their pedigree descent from Woden himself, chief of the Gods. A man's concern with his descent was concern at his place within society. The early Anglo-Saxon leaders were elected, and any man who could prove he was a descendant of the founder of a royal dynasty was entitled to stake his claim. This was a situation that led to much bloodshed amongst the settling Germanic tribesmen and in the early years of the Heptarchy. In time it gave way to the less disruptive custom of formally electing the king's eldest son. But there were exceptions, such as the election of Alfred as King of Wessex in 871 in preference to Ethelred's young son. The introduction of the Ecclesiastical Coronation from the Continent towards the end of the eighth century must also have stabilized and further dignified the role of kingship. Thereafter those who opposed their king ran the risk of incurring God's wrath into the bargain. And in the eleventh century it was asserted that 'A Christian king is Christ's deputy among Christian People', words which firmly establish the concept of the Divine Right of Kings in the Anglo-Saxon Christian world.

King Alfred had a thoroughly practical mind. Just as he marked off a candle for work, prayer and sleep, he ordained that out of each three months, his thanes should spend two at home looking after their own concerns and one at court looking to the needs of the country. These thanes together with younger men, not yet endowed with land, formed the basis of the king's company.

The king was also attended by a large number of permanent officials: 'dish-thanes', for instance, and 'wardrobe-thanes' and butlers, stewards and 'horse-thanes'. One does not have to look far for some of our contemporary equivalents: Mistress of the Queen's Wardrobe, Master of the Queen's Horse. There were many specialist workmen at Court, too, and the best of them highly prized and suitably rewarded:

> The goldsmith fashions a marvellous gift for one;
> many times that man tempers and decorates
> for the great king, who grants him broad acres*

Tides of men ebbed and flowed at Bamburgh, Winchester and the other seats of kings. There was the coming and going of ealdormen, the highest officials in the land and the king's representatives among the people, whose duty it was to maintain law and order, to support the bishops and further the work of the church, and to preside over the shire court. From time to time they were joined at court by a great gathering of bishops and

* Lines from 'The Fates of Men'.

36. A king sits with his council, or *witanegemot*. In this illustration from
Ælfric's *Old Testament* (11th century), the council imposes
the death penalty.

thanes, all the most important men in the country, summoned
by the king for a council (see plate 36) when he needed advice
on far-reaching matters: the imposition of taxes, or the making
of new laws, or the conclusion of treaties, or the redistribution of
land to accommodate the ever-hungry and growing church. At·
other times, the king received foreign emissaries: rulers from
Wales and Strathclyde come to acknowledge the overlordship of
the King of England; ambassadors arranging marriages into
ruling families on the Continent; distinguished scholars and
ecclesiastics paying courtesy calls on their way to the great
monasteries. And many who came brought gifts:

> perfumes such as never before had been seen in England, precious
> stones, especially emeralds, in whose greenness the reflected sun lit
> up the eyes of the onlookers with a pleasing light; many fleet horses;
> . . . a certain vase of onyx, carved with such subtle art by the engraver
> that the cornfields seemed truly to wave, the vines to bud, the forms
> of men to move, and so clear and polished that it reflected like a
> mirror the faces of those gazing on it . . .*

One of the most welcome guests at any court must have been

* Quoted by Dorothy Whitelock in *The Beginnings of English Society*.

the traveller with stories of strange events in far-off places. Two such men came to the court of Alfred while he was occupied in translating Orosius' *History of the World* from Latin into Anglo-Saxon, and the king added their tales to it. The voyage of Ohthere, a Norwegian who brought walrus tusks as a gift for the king, tells of a journey to the White Sea while Wulfstan told Alfred of a visit to Estonia at the eastern end of the Baltic where he had witnessed strange burial customs. He described scenes of gaming and drinking which resemble the wake as it is still practised in remote parts of Europe and then explained how, on the day a man was to be cremated, his possessions were distributed:

> Then they deposit it, the largest lot about one mile from the settlement, then the second largest, then the third largest, until it is all deposited within the one mile; and the smallest lot shall be nearest the settlement where the dead man lived. Then all the men who owned the swiftest horses in the land shall be assembled about five or six miles from that property. Then they all gallop towards that property; then the man who has the swiftest horse comes to the first lot and to the largest, and so one after another, until it is all won . . . and for this reason swift horses are extraordinarily precious there.

The Anglo-Saxon court was not a fixed institution. It moved wherever the king went, either to one of his estates, or else at immense expense to one of his more wealthy subjects. The king's pastimes were the same as those of the thane (see p. 68); and it was in Anglo-Saxon times that the royal forests were first staked out – great tracts of woodland such as the New Forest and Epping Forest where hunting rights were reserved for the king and all poachers were savagely punished.

The king and his company, like the thane and his retainers, loved above all to listen to the poet in the feasting-hall. For the poet was, in effect, the memory of the tribe, the court, the kingdom; a memorable half-line in *Beowulf* says that the poet 'wordhord onleac', unlocked the wordhoard. Only he knew all the traditions associated with the royal house and added to them when occasion arose. That is what the author of 'The Battle of Maldon' was doing; he was celebrating the heroism of the men of Essex so that later generations would not forget them. And in 937, when Athelstan and his brother Edmund crushed a combined army of Britons, Norsemen and Scots at Brunanburh, the court poet sang:

> Never, before this,
> were more men in this island
> slain by the sword's edge –
> as books and aged sages
> will confirm – since the far-off days
> when Angles and Saxons sailed here from the east,
> sought the Britons over the wide seas,
> since those warsmiths hammered the Welsh,
> and ambitious earls overran the land.

The poet was obviously exaggerating. But what does that matter? His aim was to glorify the royal family of Wessex, and he both succeeded in that aim and composed a memorable poem.

Because he had an important social function, considerable respect attached to the trained poet. In *Beowulf*, the poet says:

> And now and then one of Hrothgar's thanes
> who brimmed with poetry, and remembered lays,
> a man acquainted with ancient traditions
> of every kind, composed a new song
> in correct metre. Most skilfully that man
> began to sing of Beowulf's feat,
> to weave words together, and fluently
> to tell a fitting tale.

Few of those lays and ancient traditions have survived, but we do know that the contemporary poet in Ireland had seven years' training, and that at the end of it he could recite some 350 lays. Much the same must have been expected of the Anglo-Saxon poet. The vocabulary of the poet was formal; it made use of many compounds and of condensed metaphors known as kennings – thus the sea could be described as 'the whale's road' or 'the boat's path', a sail was 'a sea-garment', a sword was 'a battle-light', and a wife 'a peace-weaver'. The language of the poets, no less highly-wrought than the work of the jewellers, must have seemed to

37. A manuscript page from *Beowulf*. This is the only surviving copy; it was written down c. 1000.

Anglo-Saxons just as artificial as Spenser's language did to Eliza-
bethan ears. The difference is that the Anglo-Saxon poets were
working within an oral tradition; the greater part of their poems
were composed for the ear rather than the eye, and only subsequently written down (see plate 37).

All Old English poetry was composed in a four-stress, metric-
ally variable line, in which the third stress alliterated with the
first or second stress or with both – a strict formula that must
have evolved as an aide-memoire to the poet. So, for example:

> Hraegl min swigað þonne ic hrusan trede,
> oþþe þa wic buge oþþe wado drefe.
> Silent is my dress when I step across the earth,
> reside in my house or ruffle the waters.

This is the 'correct metre' to which the *Beowulf* poet refers; it is
impressive to listen to, pounding and stately.

There are many references in Old English poetry to the poet's
lyre (see plates 38 and 39), though we do not know how it was
tuned. So for example, in 'The Fates of Men':

> He will settle beside his harp
> at his lord's feet, and be handed treasures;
> he is always prepared to pluck strings
> with a plectrum – with that hard hopping thing
> he creates harmonies. Harpist, heart's desire!

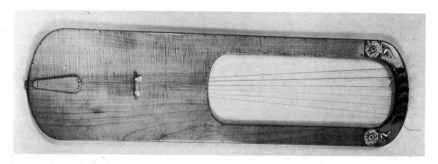

38. Reconstruction of the lyre found in the Sutton Hoo ship-burial. It is
made of maple with six pegs of poplar or willow, and measures 29¼ inches
long and 8¼ inches wide. 7th century.

39. Detail showing a harpist from the *Vespasian Psalter*. Early 8th century.

For the Anglo-Saxons poetry was both magic and everyday. It was a secret pattern of words designed to charm away evils and placate the dead, and a method of enshrining what must be remembered. It was also, as the riddles suggest, a pastime that could be shared and enjoyed by almost everyone – Cædmon (see page 110), the crow-throated cowherd, is the famous exception. There were as few people in Anglo-Saxon England unable to pick up a stringed instrument and recite a poem as there are people in England today unable to read. So perhaps we may assume that there were as many styles of recitation as there once were poets in the land.

12. One of the 'carpet pages' from the *Lindisfarne Gospels*.
c. 700.

13. A page showing The Second Coming of Our Lord
from the *Benedictional of St Æthelwold*.
Late 10th century.

RELIGION

᠍᠍🐍🐍🐍🐍🐍🐍

FATE AND THE GERMANIC GODS

🐍🐍🐍🐍🐍🐍

'FATE,' said an Anglo-Saxon poet, 'goes ever as it must.' Fate was the dark force that governed the time when a man was born, determined what would happen to him during his life, and fixed the moment of his death. The Anglo-Saxons called it *wyrd*, literally 'what will be'.

No Anglo-Saxon imagined for a moment that he could change his fate. The poet who composed 'The Wanderer' said: 'Wyrd bið ful aræd!' Fate is inexorable! And the Norsemen who settled in England were similarly aware of the Valkyries, the 'choosers of the slain' who rushed into battle on horseback, swords drawn, and selected those who must die. But, for all that, the *way* in which a man lived his life was up to him: he could ride the tide of events, face life with spirit and dignity, and be remembered and honoured for it; or else he could crumple before a seemingly meaningless destiny, and be forgotten in the dark drumroll of years. That, and that only, was the element of choice perceived by the Anglo-Saxon mind.

Despite the advent of Christianity, a sense of fate has always hovered over the North-West Europeans. There is no mistaking it in Shakespeare's lines from *King Lear*:

> As flies to wanton boys, are we to the gods;
> They kill us for their sport.

Thomas Hardy, who writes of happiness as 'but the occasional episode in a general drama of pain' ends *Tess of the d'Urbervilles* in much the same way, and a spirit of fatalism is at the heart, too, of the music of Sibelius and the plays of Ibsen. But perhaps the closing lines of 'Fern Hill' by Dylan Thomas (paradoxically a Celt) best catch the essence of the pagan Anglo-Saxon awareness of life – its transience and its possibilities:

> Oh as I was young and easy in the mercy of his means
> Time held me green and dying
> Though I sang in my chains like the sea.

The Germanic tribes who first came to England were polytheists: that is to say, they worshipped many gods. The four principal gods were Woden, god of wisdom; Tiw, god of war; Thunor, the thunder-god; and Frig, goddess of fertility. They give their names to Tuesday, Wednesday, Thursday and Friday. A goddess, Eostre, gives her name to Easter. Missionaries found it easier to 'convert' old pagan festivals – Christmas took the place of Giul (Yule) – than to impose new ones; likewise, they took over pagan temples and consecrated them to Christ.

The truth is that we know very little about the beliefs of the pagan Anglo-Saxons: but what evidence we do have from Bede, from occasional references in Old English literature and from archaeological excavation, suggests that Anglo-Saxons shared many of the beliefs of the Norsemen, whose philosophy was recorded in great detail by the great Icelandic historian, Snorri Sturluson, in his *Gylfaginning*.

According to Snorri, an after-life awaited those who led good lives and those who fell in battle. Odin (= the Anglo-Saxon Woden) had a hall with a golden roof called Gimli for the former, and for the latter another hall, Valhalla, where each night, the heroes

> feasted on pork that never gave out, and on mead which flowed instead of milk from the udders of the great goat Heidrun . . . Odin's guests spent the day in fighting, and all who fell in the combat were raised again in the evening to feast with the rest.*

* H. R. Ellis Davidson: *Gods and Myths of Northern Europe.*

The pagan Anglo-Saxons cremated their dead, and deposited their ashes in a pottery urn, such as that shown in colour plate 8. It seems reasonable to assume that whether the mourners simply left an ornament or two – a buckle, a pin, a brooch – inside the urn with the ashes, or else laid the urn amongst a wealth of treasure, they were providing for a man's possible needs in an after life.

Gylfaginning makes brilliant and breathtaking reading. Snorri describes the worlds of the gods, men and the giants (Asgard, Midgard and Jotunheim). He tells superb stories and shows how the Gods have within their own ranks, in Loki, the seed of their ultimate destruction. Loki is half-god, half-giant. He loves evil for its own sake, and causes the killing of the loved-God Baldr with an arrow of mistletoe; he sides with the giants and monsters in Ragnarök.

Ragnarök is the time when all creation rages in battle. The sea rises and engulfs the middle-earth of men; Loki launches a boat, made out of the nails of dead men, and packs it out with giants; one of Loki's children, the Midgard serpent, emerges from the sea, blowing poison; and another, the Fenris wolf, chases the sun and devours it. In the ensuing struggle between gods and men on one side, giants and monsters on the other, there are no survivors. So whatever after-life there is for men within Norse mythology is not eternal but temporal and temporary. Its fatalism is total; it must be virtually the only mythology in which the Gods are doomed to destruction.

If Anglo-Saxon mythology had been as well developed as the Norse, we might expect to find more memories of it embodied in subsequent writing. As it is, little of the jigsaw survives, but all that there is points in the same direction as the great collection of Norse traditions – towards a chilling and dark view of life.

🔊🔊🔊🔊🔊

THE GOLDEN AGE OF NORTHUMBRIA

🔊🔊🔊🔊🔊

MANY of the British driven west by the incoming Germanic tribes during the fifth and sixth centuries were Christian. They probably carried with them the tradition of how their ancestors were first converted in the second century and the story of the martyrdom of St Alban, and carried too those essentials of all early Christians, mass-books and a handful of rather dubious holy relics enshrined in a casket of wood or ivory (see plate 40). The practice of Christianity survived uninterrupted in Wales, Devon and Cornwall and in north-west England, called Strathclyde.

But cultural contact between Briton and Anglo-Saxon was extremely limited. The Anglo-Saxons came as heathens and remained heathen until twin Christian prongs – Romans from the south and Celts from the north – led to the 'reconversion' of England in the seventh century.

It was Gregory (later Pope Gregory) who saw boys with 'fair complexions, fine-cut features and fair hair'* for sale in the market place in Rome. When told that they were Angles, he replied, 'That is appropriate, for they have angelic faces, and it is right that they should become fellow-heirs with the angels in heaven.'* Gregory was appalled, though, at the paganism of the Anglo-Saxons and, when he became pope, despatched Augustine to convert them to Christianity.

Augustine reached Kent, the Kingdom of Æthelbert, in 597.

---

* Bede: *A History of the English Church and People.*

40. Panel from an early Christian casket. c. 400.

The king's Frankish wife, Bertha, was already Christian, but Æthelbert was still suspicious. In his *History of the English Church and People*, the Venerable Bede (who is the one and only great authority on Christianity in England up to about 730) wrote:

> . . . the king ordered them to remain in the island where they had landed . . . he took precautions that they should not approach him in a house, for he held an ancient superstition that if they were practisers of magical arts, they might have opportunity to deceive and master him.

But Æthelbert was impressed by Augustine's fair words and promises and allowed him to stay and 'win any people you can to your religion'.

The number of people Augustine and his monks 'won' is astonishing: on Christmas Day of that same year, 10,000 people were baptized by total immersion, following the example of the king himself. Bishoprics were established at Canterbury (for Augustine) and Rochester, and, after the subsequent conversion of Essex, in London. Augustine could not have anticipated such quick success; perhaps it was achieved too easily, for Essex soon reverted to paganism and for a while it seemed that Kent might do so too.

To find the heart of Christianity in England we must allow a generation to elapse and travel 400 miles north. King Edwin of Northumbria wanted to marry Ethelberga, daughter of Æthelbert of Kent. Promised that Edwin would not stop her from practising her faith, and with the Pope's words in her ear that 'the unbelieving husband shall be saved through the believing wife', Ethelberga set out for Bamburgh, attended by the bishop Paulinus.

In due course, Paulinus presented the case for Christianity to Edwin, and the king called a great council to discuss it. Bede recorded the moving words of one of his councillors:

> Your Majesty, when we compare the present life of man with that time of which we have no knowledge, it seems to me like the swift flight of a lone sparrow through the banqueting-hall where you sit in the winter months to dine with your thanes and counsellors. Inside there is a comforting fire to warm the room; outside, the wintry storms of snow and rain are raging. This sparrow flies swiftly in through one door of the hall, and out through another. While he is inside, he is safe from winter storms; but after a few moments of comfort, he vanishes from sight into the darkness whence he came. Similarly, man appears on earth for a little while, but we know nothing of what went before this life, and what follows. Therefore if this new teaching can reveal any more certain knowledge, it seems only right that we should follow it.

This story tells us precisely why Christianity appealed so much to the Anglo-Saxons: it offered *hope*.

So Edwin accepted Paulinus' teaching; the High Priest Coifi profaned his own altars and shrines of the idols, and the Northumbrians began their long journey from the Germanic ideal of war-service to the Christian ideal of sacrifice. The clash and reconciliation of the Germanic old and the Christian new is one of the most fascinating aspects of the Anglo-Saxon period. Rædwald, King of the East Angles, either misunderstood Christianity or was trying to get the best of both worlds when he set up a cross next to his pagan idols. A poet said 'The glories of Christ are great; fate is strongest', a conflict which was later subtly modified with the concept that fate moves in the mind of God. Another poet composed a superb poem, 'The Dream of the Rood', in which the Cross stands to Christ in the position of a retainer who has no alternative but to betray his lord, the worst of all Anglo-Saxon crimes. Perhaps the jumble on the Franks Casket (see plate 41), was typical of the knowledge of most men: a bit of Christianity, a bit of Germanic legend, and a bit of late Roman history.

Six years after his conversion in 627, King Edwin was killed fighting against the pagan Penda of Mercia allied with Cadwallon of the Welsh. Paulinus escorted Ethelberga back to Kent, many people again offered sacrifices to their old idols, and the future of Christianity in Northumbria was imperilled. But then Edwin's nephew, Oswald, defeated and killed Cadwallon, and his succession ushered in the Golden Age of Northumbria.

During his childhood, Oswald had spent several years with the dynamic monastic community on the island of Iona, which had been founded in 565 by one of the great Christian figures of all time, the Irish prince St Columba, as a base from which to convert the Scots to Christianity. It was natural enough that Oswald should now turn to the Celtic monks of Iona rather than to the Roman monks in Kent for help in restoring Christianity to his kingdom.

The Irish Christians, led by Aidan to whom Oswald gave a grant of land on the island of Lindisfarne, brought with them a tradition in many ways different to the Roman missionaries, for the Irish church had flourished as a separate entity during England's pagan centuries. Of course the message was the same: that Christ died on the Cross to save men; that there was heaven, and hell. But while the Roman church appointed bishops and priests and built churches, the Irish Christians set up virtually self-

41. Panel from the whalebone Franks Casket which was made in Northumbria in the early 8th century. These two scenes depict the Germanic hero Wayland the Smith greeting his daughter, and the Adoration of the Magi.

sufficient monasteries as a base from which monks ranged far and wide at the Abbot's discretion. And within a few years of Aidan's arrival, many new monasteries – a little group of beehive cells and a church set within some earthwork – had been founded throughout Northumbria.

The Celtic form of Christianity reflects how its monks were both in this world, mixing with all men, and out of it, living only with their own kind within the monastery. Cuthbert, a seventh-century Bishop of Lindisfarne and later patron saint of Northumbria, is a fine example. He was a sociable man; he was a fiery preacher who could bring together a group of windswept villagers and bind them with fine story-telling; he obviously loved people. And not only people: in the true Celtic tradition, many stories of his love for animals (and theirs for him) gathered around him. Bede reports how a monk saw Cuthbert stand all night in the sea, up to his neck, praying:

> At daybreak he came out, knelt down on the sand, and prayed. Then two otters bounded out of the water, stretched themselves out before him, warmed his feet with their breath, and tried to dry him on their fur. They finished, received his blessing, and slipped back to their watery home.

But this tale also reveals the other side of Cuthbert and so many other Celtic monks: he hankered after hardship, he lived a demanding ascetic life, he always needed to test himself. For this reason many monks spent months or even years (as did Cuthbert on the island of Great Farne) as solitary hermits. Plate 42 shows St Guthlac being rowed in 699 to the little island of Crowland in the Lincolnshire marshes, there to live and worship God alone. The idea of voluntary exile, too, appealed to the Celtic monks: they believed that to forgo an earthly home was to be assured of a home in heaven. That is partly why so many monks went as missionaries to Europe during the seventh and eighth centuries.

What is so attractive about the Celtic monks is their passion and their piety. They were ideally suited to be, so to speak, the shock troops, the mobile Christian missionaries who converted

42. St Guthlac is conveyed in 699 to Crowland.

Northumbria once and for all. But in 664 a momentous meeting, the Synod of Whitby, was held to thrash out the differences between the Roman and Celtic churches: not only to argue the burning issue of the day, a rather obscure business about how to work out the date of Easter, but also to size up the case for Roman diocesan as opposed to Celtic monastic Christianity. The Romans won the day and from that time until King Henry VIII's decision to defy the Pope and marry Ann Boleyn, the church in England was united.

Although some disgruntled Celtic monks returned to Iona and Ireland, the great majority stayed in their Northumbrian monasteries. And there they continued to practise the scholarly pursuits and artistic skills which, together with their zeal, had turned Northumbria in just thirty years into the nerve centre of Christianity not only in England but in Europe as a whole.

Steeped in the oral tradition, the Anglo-Saxons probably had better-developed memories than we have today. Monks doubtless knew the patter of the seven celebrations of the Divine Office: at dawn, Matins; then Prime, Tierce, Sext, Nones and Vespers; before sleeping, Compline; and at midnight, the additional service of Nocturns. Perhaps they knew by heart the 150 psalms. But they had nonetheless a great need of books (see colour plate 9) – books in which to read the scriptures and their interpretation by great scholars; from which to learn grammar, natural science, chronology, the lives of saints; and books to teach with in the monastery schools and amongst the Northumbrians.

The production of a book before the revolutionary invention of the printing press – surely the most significant invention of all time – was no light matter. It had to be copied out from an existing book letter by letter, word by word. Each monastery had its own scriptorium and during the seventh and eighth centuries Northumbrian scribes produced a steady stream of books for use both at home and abroad. A touching letter from Abbot Cuthbert of Wearmouth to a missionary on the Continent speaks of hardship that must have been common enough:

> Now truly, since you have asked for some of the works of the blessed father, for your love I have prepared what I could, with my pupils, according to our capacity . . . And if I could have done more, I would gladly have done so. For the conditions of the past winter oppressed the islands of our race very horribly with cold and ice and long and widespread storms of wind and rain, so that the hand of the scribe was hindered from producing a great number of books.*

The Roman Catholic church has always maintained that no expense or effort should be spared over objects made to the greater glory of God, and there are few greater glories than the

* *English Historical Documents, Volume I.*

Northumbrian illuminated manuscripts. Far from simply acting as copyists, the ascetic Anglo-Saxon monks decorated their manuscripts in various ways, and made them not only useful but also extremely beautiful:

> Fingers folded me and the bird's feather
> often moved over my brown surface,
> sprinkling meaningful marks; it swallowed more wood-dye
> (part of the stream) and again travelled over me
> leaving black tracks. Then a man bound me,
> he stretched skin over me and adorned me
> with gold; thus I am enriched by the wondrous work
> of smiths, wound about with shining metal.
> Now my clasp and my red dye
> and these glorious adornments bring fame far and wide
> to the Protector of Men.*

The Lindisfarne Gospels, made in the island monastery around 700, are the finest example of early Anglo-Saxon manuscript illumination, and show how three influences met and fertilized each other. At the beginning of each Gospel, the elaborate initial letter (see plate 43), sometimes occupying the better part of a page, is Celtic in origin. The portraits of the four evangelists are based on Mediterranean originals, and they are quite naturalistic, if a little stiff, compared to the delightful geometrical portrait of St Matthew in *The Book of Durrow* (see colour plate 10), which introduces the typically Celto-Saxon idea of decoration for its own sake. Thirdly, there is the native Anglo-Saxon influence: this is elaborate ribbon interlace and animal ornament so beloved of early Anglo-Saxon artists, sculptors and jewellers throughout England. The maker of *The Lindisfarne Gospels* gave over whole pages, known as 'carpet pages', to this form of ornamentation with staggering effect (see colour plate 11). The vellum pages glow with solid mineral colours – red lead, bluish-green (extracted from malachite), bright yellow (extracted from arsenic salts), and pink, blue, purple, brown and gold. The whole manu-

---

* Lines from the riddle 'Bible-Codex'

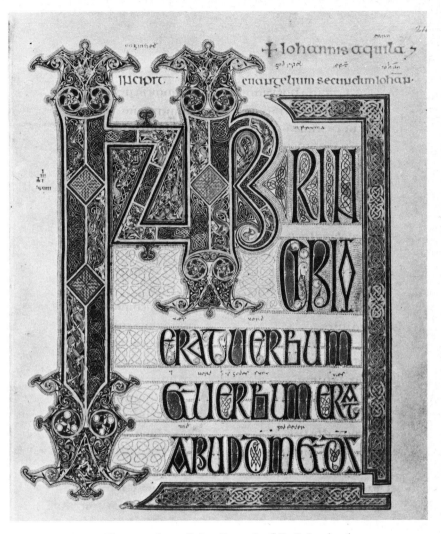

43. The opening of the Gospel of St John in the
Lindisfarne Gospels c. 700.

script is a work of controlled passion; its grand ambitious sweep
is composed of accurate attention to innumerable subtle small
designs; it is quite arguably the finest work of art ever made in
England.

Another set of influences made themselves felt in the sculptoria of the monasteries: from the Celtic world came the very idea of carving great stone crosses; from the Mediterranean came the vine-scroll decoration, which the Anglo-Saxons were quick to adopt and adapt; and from the Anglo-Saxon world came the idea of adding animals and birds to the volutions of the scroll, as in the Ruthwell Cross (see plate 44). As with manuscript illumination, so with sculpture: Mediterranean restraint yokes and beautifies the Northern passion for pure ornamentation. Men trained with hammer and chisel magnified scenes only represented hitherto on ivory casket lids, pendants, brooches. The Ruthwell Cross is a breathtaking achievement: 18 feet high, carved on all four sides and on its arms with scenes from the Gospels, 'inhabited vine scrolls', and with some of the words of 'The Dream of the Rood', the finest of the Old English religious poems:

> Listen! I will describe the best of dreams
> which I dreamed in the middle of the night
> when, far and wide, all men slept.
> I perceived a strange and lovely tree,
> most radiant, rising up before me,
> surrounded by light; it was clothed
> in gleaming gold; five precious jewels
> studded its cross-beam and many more were strewn
> around it on the earth. All the Angels of the Lord
>   protected it,
> created so fair. That was no cross of a malefactor,
> but holy spirits and men of this earth
> watched over it there . . . the entire universe.

The work produced by the sculptors of Northumbria during the seventh and eighth centuries had no equal in Europe.

In this age and place, too, the alliterative technique of the poet (see page 94) was first harnessed to Christian purposes. At the monastery of Whitby, the cowherd Cædmon who used to slink out of the hall rather than sing, was visited in a vision by a man who told him to sing. At first Cædmon refused, but the man insisted

44. Inhabited vine-scroll
on the Ruthwell Cross.
8th century.

that he should 'sing about the creation of all things'. Then Cædmon did sing:

> Nu scylun hergan   hefænricæs Uard,
> Metudes mæcti   end His modgidanc . . .
> Now we must praise the Ruler of Heaven,
> the might of the Lord and His purpose of mind,
> the work of the Glorious Father; for He,
> God Eternal, established each wonder,
> He, Holy Creator, first fashioned the heavens
> as a roof for the children of earth.
> And then our guardian, the Everlasting Lord,
> adorned this middle-earth for men.
> Praise the Almighty King of Heaven.

These are the earliest surviving lines of Anglo-Saxon poetry. C. L. Wrenn wrote:

> If this poet was, in fact, the very first to apply the Germanic heroic poetic discipline . . . to Christian and Christian edification, then indeed, the *Hymn* must be regarded . . . as a great document of poetic revolution in early Anglo-Saxon England. Whoever first applied pagan traditional poetic discipline to Christian matter set the whole tone and method of subsequent Anglo-Saxon poetry. He preserved for Christian art the great verbal inheritance of Germanic culture.*

Bede recorded the story of Cædmon. We have no reason to disbelieve him, for he was writing only sixty years after Cædmon's vision; indeed we would do well to believe him, the greatest figure in this great age. Out of a dark, tangled, superstitious time, he speaks to us in a calm, reasonable, commonsensical voice. He says, for instance: 'I have termined to elucidate meanings but express statements tersely, since plain brevity rather than prolix disputations is wont to stick in the memory.'

Bede lived from 673 until 735 in the monasteries of Wearmouth and Jarrow. He participated to the full in monastic life and, like the Abbot he lovingly describes, 'remained so humble that he

---

* C. L. Wrenn: *A Study of Old English Literature.*

loved to thresh and winnow, milk the cows and ewes, and occupied himself obediently in the bakery, garden, kitchen, and all the work of the monastery'. But with outstanding intellect and prodigious energy he also produced works on grammar and metre, commentaries on books of the Bible, scientific treatises on chronology, medicine, astronomy and meteorology, lives of the saints, and poems including a set of hymns. Above all, he wrote a four-part *History of the English Church and People*. In this work, Bede establishes the basis of historiography: he cites his sources, as 'tradition', 'ancient documents', 'my own knowledge'; he selects from and integrates the vast mass of material available to him; he invariably declares his interest and is seldom uncritical; though certainly it is true that for Bede, as for the Aran islanders of whom J. M. Synge wrote at the beginning of this century, 'the wonder is the rare expected event, like the thunderstorm or the rainbow, except that it is a little rarer and a little more wonderful.'*

Used by eighth-century missionaries on the continent, translated by King Alfred, borrowed by the Anglo-Saxon Chronicler, read and reread throughout the Middle Ages, translated both by a Catholic and a Protestant in the reign of Elizabeth I and now in the reign of the second Elizabeth acknowledged as the only great source for early Anglo-Saxon events, *A History of the English Church and People* can reasonably be described as one of the most popular histories of all time.

Even today, many people feel instinctively that Northumbria is God's own country. The simple, unselfish, often saintly, often inspired lives of many of the monks are still in the air; associations do have a way of persisting. Bede complained that in the eighth century many of the monasteries had become dissolute, and 'converted into places for eating, drinking, gossip or other amusements'. But, already, these same monasteries had made it possible to claim that the centre of European civilization – once Athens, once Rome, once Alexandria – had for the first time in history moved north of the Alps, far north, and resided in Northumbria.

* J. M. Synge: *The Aran Islands*. Mansel, Dublin and London, 1907.

ALFRED AND EDUCATION

ALFRED saved England for the English. But he was far more than a brilliant military strategist: that quality certainly won him respect and gratitude but, alone, it would barely have earned him the nickname by which he was known throughout the Middle Ages, 'Engle hirde, Engle derling', Shepherd of the English, Englishmen's darling. What did he do to deserve this? Why is he the only king we have called the Great?

For Alfred, the winning of respite from the Danes was simply a means to an end; he was anxious to restore the learning and culture that distinguished seventh and eighth-century Northumbria, and declined during the wars against the Danes. The long struggle – already so long that a man and his father and his grandfather were likely to have been caught up in it – had been extremely costly. Many of the monasteries had been destroyed; so had the cathedral schools. The Church was no longer the centre of learning, and itself too untutored to dynamize any kind of religious revival. King Alfred himself wrote:

> So completely had learning decayed in the English nation that there were very few from here to the Humber who could understand their mass-books in English, or even translate a metter from Latin into English; and I think there were not many beyond the Humber.

Part of Alfred's attempt to 'lead his clergy and people back to the learning which had once been theirs' was to make a new set of laws – a kind of moral touchstone to which anyone could refer and by which all men were to be judged. He introduced his laws in this way:

Then I, King Alfred, collected these together and ordered to be written many of them which our forefathers observed, those which I liked; and many of those which I did not like, I rejected with the advice of my councillors, and ordered them to be differently observed. For I dared not presume to set in writing at all many of my own, because it was unknown to me what would please those who should come after us.

This respect for law is an important hallmark of a civilized as opposed to a barbaric society; after all, it means that punishment is no longer arbitrary. Before Alfred, seventh and eighth century kings of Kent and of Wessex had already codified sets of laws; it is clear that Anglo-Saxon society was rather more settled than is sometimes supposed. Here is Alfred establishing the sanctity of holy ground:

Also we determine this sanctuary for every church which a bishop has consecrated: if a man exposed to a vendetta reaches it running or riding, no one is to drag him out for seven days, if he can live in spite of hunger, unless he himself fights his way out. If then anyone does so, he is liable to pay for the breach of the king's protection and of the church's sanctuary . . .

Another part of Alfred's remedy was to re-establish monasteries and monastic schools. He did so only on a very limited scale and with limited success. This was probably because there were only very few ninth-century Anglo-Saxons prepared to submit to the rigorous discipline that governed the days of the earlier Northumbrians. But Alfred also exhorted his bishops to start cathedral schools once more,

and bring it to pass, as we can very easily with God's help if we have peace, that all the young men now in England, of free men who have the means that they can apply to it, may be put to learning as long as they cannot be of use in any other employment until the time they can easily understand writing in English; afterwards one may further instruct in Latin those whom one wishes to instruct further and to promote to a higher state.

Alfred understood the power of example, and set out to make his own court a centre of education. He gathered round him a number of notable foreign ecclesiastics; one of them was Asser, a priest from the west of Wales, who served Alfred long and lived to write his biography. With the assistance of Asser and others, Alfred then set about much the most arduous part of his programme. In short, he decided that he must teach himself Latin so as to translate into Anglo-Saxon 'books which are most necessary for all men to know' (see plate 45). Alfred explained to his bishops why this had not been done before:

> I wondered exceedingly at those good learned men who were formerly throughout England and had fully studied all those books, that they did not wish to translate any part of them into their own language. But then I immediately answered myself and said: 'They did not think that men should ever become so heedless and learning so much decayed; they abstained from translation deliberately, and intended that the more wisdom there should be in the land, the more languages we knew.

So, between wars, and between bouts of some sickness that has never been satisfactorily explained, King Alfred translated five great books: Pope Gregory's *Pastoral Care* and *The Dialogues*, the former as a kind of guide-book for the clergy and the latter because it was full of stories about miracles, living proofs of the power of Christianity; *The History of the World* by Orosius and Bede's *History of the English Church and People*, to give all men a grounding in their own great past and in other historical events; and *On the Consolations of Philosophy* by Boethius, perhaps because Alfred, like the author, recognized the need to offset personal danger and human shortcoming through intellectual theory. In addition to this, Alfred also appears to have been instrumental in co-ordinating the great *Anglo-Saxon Chronicle* (see page 38).

Alfred's achievement was colossal. For most men, the labour of translating these long and complex books at all would be exacting enough. But in order to do so, Alfred had not only to teach himself Latin and wrestle with the originals; he also had to forge an Anglo-Saxon prose style capable of carrying their meaning. Before Alfred, Old English prose appears to have been limited to statements of fact, such as those abounding in the early entries in *Anglo-Saxon Chronicle*. Single-handed, he actually turned English prose into a workmanlike, flexible medium; and in so doing, he endowed England with a prose tradition for everyday use – for the writing of letters, the drawing up of charters, the making of wills – some 300 years before anywhere else in post-classical Europe.

45. Detail from the *Benedictional of St Æthelwold*. Late 10th century.

King Alfred duly sent copies of his translations to the bishops throughout his kingdom. He ends his letter to them about the lack of learning in Britain and the need for new schools with great subtlety and tact:

> And in each (book) will be a book-marker worth fifty mancuses, and I command in God's name that no-one takes the book-marker from the book or the book from the church. It is unknown how long there may be such learned bishops as now, thanks be to God, are everywhere. Therefore I wish that the books should be always at that place, unless the bishop wishes to have it with him or it is anywhere on loan or someone is copying it.

🔳🔳🔳🔳🔳

THE TENTH-CENTURY REVIVAL

🔳🔳🔳🔳🔳

ALFRED's anxiety about the decay of learning is confirmed by the dearth of surviving manuscripts or ecclesiastical ornaments from the ninth or early tenth centuries; and little that does survive compares favourably with earlier Northumbrian art. The country's first concern was with survival against the Danes. It often happens that a time of conflict is not in itself a time of great learning or artistic accomplishment, although it may engender one.

In fact the only really fine works of art from this period are also the only existing pieces of Anglo-Saxon embroidery: St Cuthbert's stole and maniple. The veneration of Cuthbert (see page 105), for whom Durham Cathedral was built between 1093 and 1104 as a final resting-place, increased from year to year after his death because his body remained uncorrupt. It is easier to scoff than to explain why; perhaps his body was in some way embalmed. From time to time, his lovely, simple wooden coffin (see plate 46) was opened to check that there was no hoax. On one such occasion the early tenth-century maniple and stole (see colour plate 12) must have been put into it. The colours have partly faded now, but once the rather primitive but elegant portrait of St Peter, surrounded by acanthus leaves, glowed pink and brown, blue and green against a glittering gold background. Anglo-Saxon embroidery had a high reputation throughout Europe; this one example gives us some idea why.

There was no quick return for Alfred's effort; it was two generations after his death before there was a renewed hunger

46. Part of the late 7th century oak lid of St Cuthbert's coffin.
The figure of Christ is incised on it.

for the monastic life. But then, for the second time, there followed a period of intense artistic activity. This time its heart was in Wessex, the one part of England to remain free of the Vikings. Much of the art produced at this time is known as the work of the 'Winchester School', but this does not necessarily mean it was produced at Winchester itself: only that it shared a common influence. This influence was Carolingian: that is, artists who had worked at the court of Charlemagne, who themselves had been influenced by the work of earlier Northumbrian manuscripts, taken over to the Frankish court by such missionaries as Alcuin, director of Charlemagne's monastic school at Aix-en-Provence. What we find in the Winchester School is, once more, a love of ornament for its own sake, with the stiff acanthus leaf (as in St Cuthbert's stole) taking the place of the ribbon interlace and the vine-scroll motif; and also the exciting introduction of natural rather than stylized portraiture of the human figure, an influence which Carolingian artists had derived from the Byzantine world.

47. Ivory panel only three inches high from Winchester, 10th century.

The figures are often rather clumsy, especially in the stone sculpture of this period. One wishes that substantial wall-painting survived, for we know that many churches were alight with great colourful murals. Perhaps the best sculptural portraiture was achieved in miniature work, such as the ivory panel (see plate 47) found in Winchester. Only three inches high, it is graceful, realistic and satisfying as a design.

The finest achievement of the Winchester School artists, like those in Northumbria, was in manuscript illumination. One most attractive style took its lead from the ninth century *Utrecht Psalter* in Rheims: the figures are breathless, they have nervous energy, and give the appearance of being swiftly and simply drawn; they look curiously oriental. Comparison of a detail from an Anglo-Saxon psalter made about AD 1,000 with a page from the *Utrecht Psalter* shows how the Anglo-Saxon artist has both imitated the original and added a charming, humorous touch of his own (see plates 48 and 49).

Perhaps the most outstanding manuscript of this period is the

48. Detail from the *Utrecht Psalter*. 9th century.

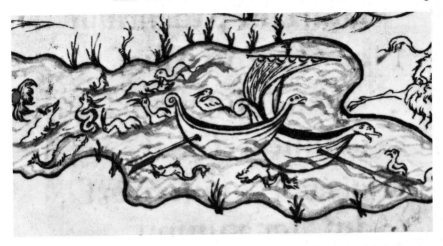

49. Detail from the *Harley Psalter*. c. 1000. Note how the bird on the boat's prow is talking to the duck.

Benedictional of St Æthelwold; written in about 980, this book of blessings is accompanied by drawings of figures, often within architectural settings, surrounded by great borders of acanthus. These illuminations combine the static and the restless in a most exciting way, and make full use of a rich palette of colours – many pastel shades, and red, blue, green, purple, gold. What is there more striking in Anglo-Saxon art than the portrait of The Second Coming of our Lord? The authoritative, graceful figure of Christ (see colour plate 13) seems to be walking out of the oval cameo as if travelling onward: the exile come home.

During the tenth and eleventh centuries, the Anglo-Saxons built a great many stone churches, and many still survive – a few intact and unadulterated, most with later additions. Perhaps the most characteristic and impressive feature of the Anglo-Saxon church is its sheer solidity. It keeps its feet on the ground; it is commonsensical; it does not aspire, like the brilliant work of the medieval builders. This is true of the seventh-century church out on the marshes at Bradwell-on-Sea in Essex (see plate 50), built by the saintly Northumbrian missionary, Cedd; it is a tough, uncompromising, bleak fist of a building that 1,300 years have failed to unclench. It is equally true of the more welcoming tenth-century tower of Earls Barton church in Northamptonshire (see plate 51) which many call the finest surviving piece of Anglo-Saxon architecture. But here the austerity is offset by some typical adornment: pilaster strips running vertically up the walls, giving the illusion of additional height; horizontal strips, reinforcing the sense of volume; semi-circular arcading (above the first horizontal strip) and two rows of triangular arcading (above the second) by way of decoration. Other characteristics of late Anglo-Saxon architecture are little triangular windows, mid-wall shafts, and so-called 'long and short work', which consists of stones set alternately upright and horizontal at the quoins: that is, where wall meets wall.

50. The church of St Peter-on-the-Wall at Bradwell-on-Sea in Essex. This was the first cathedral of the East Saxons. 7th century.

One picture in the *Benedictional of St Æthelwold*, which was never finished by the illuminator, shows Æthelwold himself blessing a congregation from the door of the new cathedral at Win-

51. Earl's Barton church, Northamptonshire.

chester which he had rebuilt in 980 (see plate 52). From it, we
see that at least some churches had a bell, and also a weathercock:

> My breast is puffed up and my neck is swollen.
> I've a fine head and a waving tail,
> ears and eyes also but only one foot . . .
> Scourged by the rainlash, I stand alone;
> I'm bruised by heavy batteries of hail,
> hoar-frost attacks and snow half-hides me.
> I must endure all this, not pour out my misery.

Another adornment on some churches was a sundial, such as
that at St Gregory's Minster in Kirkdale, Yorkshire (see plate
53). The surrounding inscription tells how the church was rebuilt
and the words on the dial itself, which is divided into eight
sections, translates, 'This is day's Sun marker at every tide.'

Outside Wessex, the predominant artistic influence during the
tenth century was not Carolingian but Norse. A great many stone
crosses continued to be hewn. Like the earlier ones, they teem
with animal ornament and the vine-scroll motif. But they are no
longer graceful; they are coarse, though sometimes redeemed by
sheer vigour. This form of decoration is called Jellinge, the name
of the court of Danish kings in Jutland where the style is also
found.

A rather similar Anglo-Norse style, Ringerike, sometimes
makes use of the acanthus leaf found in the Winchester School.
One of the best examples of this style is the tombstone (see plate
54) found in the churchyard of St Paul's Cathedral in London, a
cultural crossroads then as now. The animal has a controlled
wildness; it was originally painted with white spots, just as the
boar on the Benty Grange helmet (plate 8) had silver studs, and
the rest of the tombstone was painted in two or three colours.

There is plenty of evidence of artistic endeavour throughout
the Danelaw; but whether it be sculpture, metalwork or any
other artistic discipline, the level of attainment never approxi-
mates to the Golden Age of Northumbria or to the Winchester
School.

52. Page from the *Benedictional of St Æthelwold*. Late 10th century. Note the bells and weathercocks.

53. Sundial at St Gregory's Minster in Kirkdale, Yorkshire. c. 1055.

The monastic revival stimulated not only artistic but also scholarly achievement. Most important was the development of religious literature intended both for the monks in their cloisters and for the eyes and ears of any Christian layman.

Ælfric was born in 955, educated by Bishop Æthelwold in Winchester and given charge of the monastic school at Cerne Abbas in Dorset before becoming Abbot of Eynsham in Oxfordshire. It was he who developed what Alfred had begun, the use of Anglo-Saxon as a language for the expression of ideas rather than simply a tool for recording events, laws, and the like. He combined a strong sense of grammatical precision with an awareness of the old power of alliteration, and was the first Englishman to write prose with evident ease. With clear mind and burning sincerity, he wrote lives of the saints, such as that of Edmund (see page 48); he translated the first books of the Bible, the Pentateuch; he wrote 120 sermons; and his lively and charming *Colloquy*, with its dialogue between teacher and pupils about different kinds of work, was widely used in the monastic schools. Ælfric was recognized as the leading intellect and communicator of his time – a man prepared to share his gifts with other men, as we can see from his enormously wide range of correspondence;

54. Ringerike tombstone found in the graveyard of St. Paul's Cathedral, London. 10th or 11th century.

and full of understanding and tenderness for the young boys in monastic schools for whom he wrote both the *Colloquy* and his Latin *Grammar*, which he introduces with the disarming admission that learning Latin may seem tedious but that his book will be 'a certain beginning if it is pleasing to anyone'.

The idea of the sermon as literature, so unappealing to most twentieth-century minds, was further developed by the fiery Wulfstan, Archbishop of York. He was less stylish and scholarly but more passionate than Ælfric. For the best known of his works, he took a pseudonym based on part of his own name, and laid into his countrymen with a violent denunciation of their misdeeds. *Sermo Lupi ad Anglos* is repetitive to the point of mono-

CONCLUSION

THE poet Keith Douglas who was killed during World War II wrote:

> Remember me when I am dead
> and simplify me when I'm dead.

This book tries to simplify the Anglo-Saxons, our ancestors, so as to discover what was essential to them and about them. How much is their sensibility part of our sensibility?

After the Battle of Hastings, Norman French became the language of the ruling caste. For 300 years it remained so, and the words of an unknown twelfth-century poet indicate how keenly the subjugation was felt:

> Now is this teaching abandoned and the people is lost.
> Now it is men of other languages that teach our people,
> And many of the teachers are damned and the people as well.

And yet in about 1350, thanks to the sheer strength and flexibility of the language and the number of ordinary folk who continued to speak it, English re-emerged as first language, now enriched with a French vocabulary, and for the first time since the Conquest, major works of literature were produced in England: *Piers Plowman, Sir Gawain and the Green Knight,* and *The Canterbury Tales.* The words in this book, and the language you and I use each time we open our mouths, is at least fifty per cent Anglo-Saxon in origin.

Beowulf and a number of the shorter Old English poems celebrate heroism – a most unfashionable quality. Listen to the words of Leofsunu at the Battle of Maldon:

> I give you my word that I will not retreat
> one inch; I shall forge on
> and avenge my lord in battle.
> Now that he has fallen in the fight
> no loyal warrior living at Sturmere
> need reproach me for returning home lordless
> in unworthy retreat, for the weapon shall take me,
> the iron sword.

The will to win and yet the willingness to look defeat in the eye is characteristic of the Anglo-Saxons and characteristic of the English today. The same spirit that informs the lines above characterized Churchill's speeches during the Second World War. And what about the reserve, the doggedness, the stubbornness, and the strength of purpose that form part of the English make-up? It is all too easy to oversimplify; but we can all, out of our own experience, think of people who embody these attitudes and events that typify them. It can be argued that it is precisely these qualities in peacetime that make for heroism in war: the refusal to be shaken off. The Old English poems are thick with references to the stoicism that underlies these attributes. Is it altogether absurd to compare Beowulf telling Hrothgar

> Shoulder your sorrows in silence this day;
> this is what I expect of you

with the characteristically gloomy good cheer of a frustrated crowd? And does the ironical humour that frustration, and worse, always produce not have its own echo in the Anglo-Saxon love of understatement? At the moment, for instance, when those who stay to fight at Maldon will clearly die, the poet comments laconically: 'Then those who did not wish to be there left the battlefield.' This grim humour is characteristic of the Icelandic sagas too. And in *Gylfaginning*, Snorri Sturluson describes the binding of the fearful Fenris wolf by the Gods with a magical ribbon. The wolf says:

'I don't want to have that ribbon put on me. But rather than be accused of cowardice by you, let one of you place his hand in my mouth as a pledge that this is done in good faith.' Each of the gods looked at the other then and thought that they were in a fix, and not one of them would stretch forth his hand, until Tyr put out his right hand and laid it in the wolf's mouth. Now when the wolf began to struggle against it, the band tightened, and the more fiercely he struggled the firmer it got. Then all laughed except Tyr; he lost his hand.

The fatalism of the Anglo-Saxons is echoed in a number of North-West European writers and composers. Their sense of melancholy and nostalgia is arguably even more pervasive. Here are ten lines from the anonymous elegy, probably composed in the ninth century, 'The Seafarer':

He who is accustomed to the comforts of life
and, proud and flushed with wine, suffers
little hardship living in the city,
will never know how I, heavy with weariness,
have often had to make the ocean paths my home.
The night-shadow grew long, it snowed from the north,
frost fettered the earth; hail, coldest of grain,
battered the ground. But now my blood
is stirred that I should make trial
of the mountainous streams, the tossing salt waves . . .

And here are six by Wordsworth:

What though the radiance which was once so bright
Be now forever taken from my sight,
Though nothing can bring back the hour
Of splendour in the grass, or glory in the flower;
We will grieve not, rather find
strength in what remains behind . . .

Is there not common to both a determination to make do, combined with an ache for all that is lost? One does not have to look far for further examples: Gray's 'Elegy in a Country Churchyard', for instance. That poem is always held up as utterly English; certainly its sense of gentle melancholy is as old as the earliest poems written in our language.

The melancholy in Anglo-Saxon poetry is often allied to wonder at the mysterious and beautiful in nature. This is true of the Riddles: in 'Sun and Moon' the sun retrieves its light from the fleeing moon that escapes over the horizon as day dawns:

> Dust lifted to heaven; dew fell on the earth,
> Night fled hence; and no man knew
> Thereafter, where that strange creature went.

It is true of the elegies, and of parts of *Beowulf*:

> These two live
> in a little-known country, wolf-slopes, windswept headlands,
> perilous paths across the boggy moors, where a mountain stream
> plunges under the mist-covered cliffs,
> rushes through a fissure. It is not far from here,
> if measured in miles, that the lake stands,
> shadowed by trees stiff with hoar-frost.
> A wood, firmly-rooted, frowns over the water,

As one might expect of an island race, we can also certainly claim for both Anglo-Saxons and Celts an acute awareness of the sea, 'the flint-grey rollers' racing to the shore, perfectly summed up in John Masefield's line:

> I must go down to the seas again, to the lonely sea and the sky

One or both parts of this combination of melancholy and wonder at the natural world is fundamental to the work of countless artists: some of the music of Delius, Vaughan Williams, Bax, John Ireland; the paintings of Samuel Palmer (see plate 55), Constable and Turner; the poems of John Clare, Edward Thomas.

55. 'Valley thick with Corn' by Samuel Palmer.

The Anglo-Saxons loved ornament and ceremony. Their poems were highly wrought; their illuminated manuscripts are formal masterpieces; entertainment in the hall was the enactment of a time-honoured ritual. Love of ritual militates against sudden change. The Anglo-Saxons were, when all is said and done, a quite extraordinarily conservative people. Their society was rigidly stratified; their attitudes changed very, very little during the 600 years between their first arrival in England and the Battle of Hastings. That was a kind of strength; it was also a weakness – indeed it is because their military tactics were outmoded at Hastings that they lost that battle.

How much do we care today about ritual? Who watched, for instance, the last great royal occasion? Who was quite unimpressed by all the pomp and ceremony, that changes so little from generation to generation? Why does Britain have a monarchy and not a republic? A rite is 'a formal procedure or act in a religious or otherwise solemn observance'; and it may be that a conscious and unconscious love of ritual, and all that implies in terms of insulation and conservatism, is the greatest legacy of the Anglo-Saxons.

If we are to achieve the best perspective, we must not think of Britain as isolated; it has never been so. 'The Seafarer' says

> My mind roves with the waves
> over the whale's domain, it wanders far and wide
> across the face of the earth, return again to me
> eager and unsatisfied.

Our minds can be like his. We should attempt to make comparisons not simply between the Anglo-Saxons and the twentieth-century English but between the pre-Conquest Germanic peoples and the North-West Europeans and North Americans of today. As I look around at the way we lead our lives and the works of art we produce, there seem to be fairly obvious links between present and past. This should not be a matter for surprise; it should be a challenge and an incentive. We need to look back to look forward.

꘡꘡꘡꘡꘡꘡

BIBLIOGRAPHY

꘡꘡꘡꘡꘡꘡

I. SOURCE MATERIAL IN TRANSLATION

Alexander, Michael. *The Earliest English Poems*. Penguin, Harmondsworth, 1966. Bilingual edition, University of California Press, Berkeley, 1970

Anglo-Saxon Chronicle, The. A Revised Translation edited by Dorothy Whitelock. Eyre and Spottiswoode, London, 1961

Bede. *A History of the English Church and People*. Translated with an Introduction by Leo Sherley-Price. Penguin, Harmondsworth, 1955

Clancy, Joseph P. *The Earliest Welsh Poetry*. Macmillan, London, 1970

Crossley-Holland, Kevin. *The Battle of Maldon and Other Old English Poems*. Introductions by Bruce Mitchell. Macmillan, London, 1965. St. Martin's Press, New York, 1967. *Beowulf*. Introduced by Bruce Mitchell. Macmillan, London, 1968. Farrar, Straus & Giroux, New York, 1968. *Storm and Other Old English Riddles*. Macmillan, London, 1970. Farrar, Straus & Giroux, New York, 1970

English Historical Documents : Volume I, c. 500–1042. Edited by Dorothy Whitelock. Eyre and Spottiswoode, London, 1955. Oxford University Press, New York, 1955

Gordon, R. K. *Anglo-Saxon Poetry*. Dent, London, 1926. Dutton, New York.

Magnusson, Magnus and Pálsson, Hermann. *King Harald's Saga*. Penguin, Harmondsworth, 1966 *Njal's Saga*. Penguin, Harmondsworth, 1960. *The Vinland Sagas*. Penguin, Harmondsworth, 1965

Sturluson, Snorri. *The Prose Edda*. Selected and translated by Jean I. Young. University of California Press, Berkeley and Los Angeles, 1971

2. NON-FICTION FOR THE SAME AGE GROUP

Clancy, Joseph P. *Pendragon: Arthur and His Britain*. Macmillan, London, 1971. Praeger, New York, 1971

Denny, Norman and Filmer-Sankey, Josephine. *The Bayeux Tapestry*. Collins, London, 1966. Atheneum, New York, 1966

Grohskopf, Bernice. *From Age to Age: Life and Literature in Anglo-Saxon England*. Atheneum, New York, 1968

Quennell, Marjorie and C. H. B. *Everyday Life in Anglo-Saxon Times* (originally part of *Everyday Life in Anglo-Saxon, Viking and Norman Times*). Carousel, London, 1972

Sellman, R. R. *The Anglo-Saxons*. Methuen, London, 1959. Roy, New York

3. FICTION FOR THE SAME AGE GROUP

Crossley-Holland, Kevin. *The Sea-Stranger*. Heinemann, London, 1973. Seabury Press, New York, 1974. *The Fire-Brother*. Heinemann, London, 1975. Seabury Press, New York, 1975. *The Earth-Father*. Heinemann, London, 1976

Green, Roger Lancelyn. *The Myths of the Norsemen*. Bodley Head, London, 1962 and Puffin, Harmondsworth, 1970

Hodges, C. Walter. *The Namesake*. George Bell, London, 1964 and Puffin, Harmondsworth, 1967. Coward, McCann & Geoghegan, New York, 1964. *The Marsh King*. George Bell, London, 1967 and Puffin, Harmondsworth, 1970

Kingsley, Charles. *Hereward the Wake*. Everyman (Dent), and many other editions. Everyman (Dutton), New York, 1909

Nye, Robert. *Bee-Hunter*. Faber, London, 1968

Stanley-Wrench, Margaret. *The Silver King*. World's Work, Kingswood, 1968.

Sutcliff, Rosemary. *The Sword at Sunset*. Hodder, London, 1963. *Dawn Wind*. Oxford University Press, London, 1961. Henry Z. Walck, New York, 1973. *The Shield Ring*. Oxford University Press, London, 1956. Henry Z. Walck, New York, 1972. *Dragon-Slayer: The Story of Beowulf*. Puffin, Harmondsworth, 1970

Trease, Geoffrey. *Mist over Athelney*. Macmillan, London, 1958

Treece, Henry. *The Eagles have Flown*. Bodley Head, London, 1970. *Hounds of the King*. Bodley Head, London, 1971.

Walsh, Jill Paton and Crossley-Holland, Kevin. *Wordhoard*. Macmillan, London, 1969 and Puffin, Harmondsworth, 1971. Farrar, Straus and Giroux, New York, 1969

4. WIDER READING

Barber, Richard. *King Arthur in Legend and History*. Cardinal Books, London, 1973. Rowman & Littlefield, Totowa, New Jersey, 1974

Chadwick, Nora. *The Celts*. Penguin, Harmondsworth, 1970. Peter Smith, Gloucester, Massachusetts

Davidson, H. Ellis. *Gods and Myths of Northern Europe*. Penguin, Harmondsworth, 1964

Frere, Sheppard. *Britannia*. Routledge and Kegan Paul, London, 1967. Harvard University Press, Cambridge, 1967

Hodgkin, R. H. *A History of the Anglo-Saxons*. Third Edition. Two volumes. Oxford University Press, London, 1952. Oxford University Press, New York, 1953

Hoskins, W. G. *The Making of the English Landscape*. Hodder and Stoughton, London, 1955 and Penguin, Harmondsworth, 1970. Peter Smith, Gloucester, Massachusetts

Jones, Gwyn. *A History of the Vikings*. Oxford University Press, London, 1968. Oxford University Press, New York, 1968

Leeds, E. T. *Early Anglo-Saxon Art and Archaeology*. Clarendon, Oxford and London, 1936. Oxford University Press, New York, 1936

Stenton, F. M. *Anglo-Saxon England*. Second Edition. Clarendon, Oxford and London, 1947. Third edition, Oxford University Press, New York, 1971

Thomas, Charles. *Britain and Ireland in Early Christian Times*. Thames and Hudson, London, 1971. McGraw-Hill, New York, 1971

Thorpe, Lewis. *The Bayeux Tapestry and the Norman Invasion*. The Folio Society, London, 1973

Whitelock, Dorothy. *The Beginnings of English Society*. Penguin, Harmondsworth, 1952

Wilson, D. M. *The Anglo-Saxons*. Thames and Hudson, London, 1960

INDEX